THE
SEASONS
OF OUR
GRIEF

Embracing the Journey

DR. RAY MITSCH

MEDIA.COM

Published by
Illumify Media Global
www.IllumifyMedia.com
"Let's bring your book to life!"

Paperback ISBN: 978-1-959099-50-5

Cover design by Debbie Lewis

Printed in the United States of America

CONTENTS

ACKNOWLEDGMENTS

Where do you begin to recognize the people who had a significant role in the creation of such a book? Quite honestly, it is impossible to do, but that doesn't mean that they don't deserve some mention of the important roles they have played in the inspiration, support, and confidence in me to write a book like this.

This book has been thirty years in the making. My last book on grief was completed in 1993. A lot of history, losses, and experiences have accumulated during the last three decades of my life. That is what you will find in a book like this. It is a distillation, a collection of hard-learned wisdom.

One of the greatest groups of teachers I have had in my life are the devoted and faithful students I have had walk through my classes since I started teaching at Colorado Christian University. Their vulnerability and willingness to explore the hardest places of their lives have been nothing short of inspiring and profound. In trusting me as their teacher, they have taught me how life is seen from their unique perspective, and it is for them that I have written this book.

This book has also been inspired by my eldest daughter who walked through a loss, in which I played a part and which was the impetus for this book. In fact, this book was originally proposed in 2009 because of her struggle to hang on to the truth in the face of significant losses. Her courage, honesty, beauty and willingness to accept the offer of her Abba to retreat back into His arms were nothing short of miraculous, courageous and humbling. As a result, you have a book informed by her human story of loss, struggle, and redemption.

Finally, and by no means the least to be mentioned, has to be to my long-suffering wife (because she married a dreamer) and lifelong friend, Linda, who was the strongest voice in persisting and encouraging me not to give up on bringing this story to life. She has been joined by two friends in Dr. Bill Saxby (who wrote the foreword for this book) and Dr. Ed Smyth who have been and continue to be devoted, encouraging friends and played a significant role in supporting me as I completed this project. It has been birthed in fits and starts and even restarts, and I pray that it will encourage, empower, inspire, and provide the reader with a personal guide for the process of grief.

FOREWORD

In 2005 I asked my administrative assistant if she knew of any potential faculty applicants who could teach in the MA counseling program that I was directing. She mentioned that her teaching pastor was also a counseling psychologist in private practice at a Christian faith-based practice located nearby. I interviewed Dr. Ray Mitsch and hired him to teach as an affiliate (adjunct) faculty in the program. Over the next few years, Ray taught several of the MA counseling courses with subsequent feedback from students that included, "He hears me," "He cares," "He knows his area," "He loves the Lord." In 2008 I was looking for a full-time faculty member to teach in the traditional undergraduate psychology major at Colorado Christian University (CCU) where I was then a dean. I again turned to Ray and offered him the position. Ray has been an exemplary colleague, friend, and brother throughout the ensuing years. Student and peer feedback remains glowing.

Early in his career as a professor, he developed a course entitled Grief and Loss that relied upon his earlier publication with Lynn Brookside, *Grieving the Loss of Someone you Love: Daily Meditations to Help You Through the Grieving Process* (2014). While it was not a required course for the CCU psychology major and was scheduled during the winter term, it became such a popular course that it soon required two sections when periodically offered with students across many majors enrolling. Ray has not only lived through grief and loss, but he has also taught hundreds of students about the process. Currently, each spring semester we offer two large sections of the Grief and Loss course, which now includes a small group experience so that students can directly address their own grieving and losses.

The book you have in your hands is the result of the many hours Ray has spent teaching and mentoring students and other adults about the seasons of grief. He takes a narrative perspective as opposed to the more traditional stages-of-grief model without negating the wisdom developed from that model, but rather by incorporating it, making it come alive. Telling one's story is akin to being there, quietly listening to each person and the throes one may go through as they journey through life. "Seasons of Our Grief", with its narrative vignettes, lets the reader see into the windows of the heart as each of the characters moves through the seasons. The reader easily enters the life of the characters with the many ebbs and flows of grief, traversing the familiar territory with the many vicissitudes of grief and loss.

My hope and prayer is that while on this journey with the people you will listen to and form a community with, you will be transformed into one who will not shy away from the grief and loss you or those in your circle of community have or will have felt. May you be blessed as you enter the journey that awaits you.

Bill Saxby, PhD
Professor of Psychology and Dean Emeritus
Colorado Christian University

INTRODUCTION

Grief and grieving is messy. As a matter of fact, if it is anything but messy, one must wonder what is going on with the person grieving. Over the course of many generations, humanity's approach to grief and loss has changed often, at times dramatically. At one point in our history, death, dying and grieving were seen as a natural part of life. As a matter of fact, it has only been relatively recently that we have created such a chasm between life and death that many people see death as the ultimate inconvenience interrupting their pursuit of fulfillment and happiness.

A WINDOW FOR THE SOUL

What you have before you is a series of windows through which you can watch, listen, and think with two specific people as they traverse their journeys of grief and the seasons of their grief. Because the grief we experience as humans is an intensely personal one. Rather than try to "teach" you the reader about grief, it makes more sense to give you an opportunity to shadow two young people as they try to "work out" their grief in the uniqueness of their separate situations. In that way, you don't have in your hands an manual on grief and grieving but rather an invitation to join two people as they struggle with their grief, finding different solutions, different views, and ultimately the healing that they each seek but a healing that often surprises them in its appearance.

When it comes to experiences that we have rarely (if ever) experienced before, we tend to search for the way to do it "right." The temptation in reading a book like this is to transform its narrative into a formula for your own life and experiences. While there is a relative certainty and predictability to that, it negates the personal nature of processing our own grief. No one shares our history, no one *knows* our history (only we do), and therefore, attempting to apply these vignettes to our own specific situation will deny the importance and depth of what *we* are experiencing. There is an important aspect of our search for an "answer" to our grief, and that is exactly what interferes with "working through" our grief. Grief's specificity to each of us can be maddening, and at the same time it is a necessary connection to our unique experiences as humans.

The approach to managing and controlling life that is described above is the very thing that interferes and undermines our journey through grief. It's our desire for the "right way" to do grief rather than "our way" to do grief. It feels isolating and lonely to be out there without any markers, but it is encouraging to link arms with others who have walked through this journey too. The key is that those "others" are not attempting to tell you how to do it, but instead displaying the willingness to walk with you through it, respecting and honoring the fact that your journey may not be like theirs. There are various individuals walking alongside the main characters in the two accounts in this book, who will display either a respect for the journey the main characters are walking or succumb to the temptation to tell them how to do grief in order to help them feel better and recover more quickly. In spite of what we may have learned, speed is not the issue or of prime importance. Commitment and patience instead are the key to thorough healing.

Part of your challenge, therefore, is not only to walk the journey with each character but also to take note of the seasons they go through. The characteristics of each season have been written into their stories, and the attempts the characters make to fashion the appropriate tools for each are just as important. After the account of each person's struggle or situation, you will find the author highlighting for you the aspects of the season and the tools that you can begin to use yourself.

EMBRACING OUR HUMANITY

Finally, because I'm firmly convinced that we are made in the image of God, and that image carries with it a desire for community, this book represents an invitation into community and friendship with the characters in it. Grief is to be experienced, wrestled, and fought out in the context of community, which is what we were designed for. The isolation and disconnection in matters of grief are the major contributors to the superficiality we experience in many of our relationships. Our lives are built on contrasts in which each experience or emotion gives meaning to its opposite. Sadness gives meaning to joy, and grief gives meaning to life. That tension between the reality of death and life is what you are being invited into through the pages of this book.

In a scene from *Shadowlands*, the retelling of the story of the love affair between C.S. Lewis and Joy Grisham, the two spend their belated honeymoon at an inn in the country. As part of their stay they take a drive into the countryside. On a walk they are caught in a rainstorm in which they seek refuge from the rain in a nearby barn. Listen to the conversation.

"It's not going to last, Jack," Joy says, looking at Lewis while leaning on her cane.

"We shouldn't think about that now, let's not . . . spoil the time we have together," Lewis says, looking wistfully away across the countryside and shifting uncomfortably against the column of the barn.

Joy persists. "It doesn't spoil it, it makes it real." The thunder cracks, seeming to underscore what Joy just said. "Let me say just say it before the rain stops and we go back." Joy shifts from leg to leg using her cane to distribute her weight and in obvious pain.

"What is there to say?" Lewis wipes the rain from his face while he turns to her.

"That I'm going to die. And I want to be with you then too. The only way I can do that is if I'm able to talk to you about it now." Joy's intensity and bluntness underscored the importance and gravity of what she was communicating.

"I'll manage somehow, don't worry about me," Lewis says, looking away.

"No, . . . it can be better than that. I think it can be better than just managing. What I'm trying to say is" she pauses to gather her thoughts, "the pain then is part of the happiness now." She looks at Lewis expectantly, but with immense compassion for the impact of her words on him.

Lewis is clearly dumfounded by what she has just said, and all he can do is move toward her as she smiles back at him.

"It's the deal . . . ," she says with an air of inevitability and acceptance.[1]

This interaction between Joy and Lewis captured by the movie underscores the driving force behind writing this book. Our approach to grief and grieving has robbed us (with our full and unknowing cooperation and complicity) of the full richness of being human and experiencing depth in our relationships. My hope is that the richness of grief will be captured in these pages, and perhaps in some small way a measure of courage will be gained by walking with the characters facing the fullness of their and our humanity to find the depth for which God designed us to connect.

1

NUMBNESS

"Here is one of the worst things about having someone you love
die: It happens again every single morning."
—Anna Quindlen

Joy didn't know *what* to think. It was bad enough that her boyfriend abandoned her at the news that she was pregnant, but the pregnancy had been pretty uneventful other than the fact that she had to do it alone. She had made the choice to keep the baby against all input from family and friends to the contrary. After seeing the ultrasound, she simply couldn't deny the fact that what she was seeing was a living human being who was vulnerable and worthy of being protected and nurtured.

She had experienced the joys of feeling movement for the first time, watching a little appendage traverse the inside of her belly that was increasing in size with each passing week. As time passed, she had grown in her love for this little one, and with each passing week she grew more and more excited to lay her eyes on her child.

Then over the course of a few weeks, she became aware of the fact that the activity in her belly seemed to grow less and less, until finally it stopped altogether. She didn't understand what was going on; everything had been fine only a few weeks ago. Panicked and worried, she hastily made an appointment to see the obstetrician. On the day of the appointment, she sat in the examination room waiting for the doctor to appear and find out what was going on.

"Hi, Joy, what seems to be going on?" the doctor asked.

"Something really strange is going on right now, Dr. Miller. All movement has stopped in my belly. I don't understand what is going on. The baby has had times of quiet, and even was on schedule with me when I slept. But lately there's been no movement at all."

Dr. Miller furrowed her brow and moved rather quickly to get the ultrasound equipment set up. She prepared to listen to Joy's belly, and her face gave nothing away that something might be wrong.

As she began the ultrasound, Joy realized that something was really different. There was no heartbeat that had been so comforting to hear on the other occasions that she had been in the office. Dr. Miller continued her examination with little emotion. She felt Joy's belly, attempting to discover the placement of the baby, but the lack of movement continued.

Dr. Miller finally spoke. "Joy, I can come to no other conclusion but that your baby has died in utero. There are many reasons for this . . ."

Joy felt the world instantaneously come to an abrupt halt. She could feel nothing. The doctor continued to talk, explaining the reasons for a stillbirth and reviewing the procedures they would need to consider to facilitate a delivery. It was as if the doctor was speaking another language and was miles away. Joy knew tears were streaming down her face, but she couldn't feel them. It was like she was living in two different universes. One that you know is reality and the other where everything is foggy, muffled, and indistinct.

Joy's parents were amazing in the days that followed. They helped her to make the decision about inducing labor and were with her every step of the process. Joy gave birth to a little baby boy who had the umbilical cord wrapped around his neck. After they cleaned him up after the birth, she was amazed at how beautiful he was in spite of the fact that he had died a month before. She decided to name him Aaron after her dad.

There were really no words to describe what she was feeling as the days turned into weeks. Her life felt like it had lost its anchor and she was cast adrift on an endless sea with no horizon, nothing to help her chart a course. All she really wanted to do was stay in bed and cocoon herself in her blankets and hope that life would end. Numbness was all she felt, if someone could actually "feel" numbness. It was more like a sense of nothingness.

One day Joy had a visitor. Her mom had invited a friend to come over and spend some time with Joy. Her name was Meg, and she seemed nice enough. She had a way about her that was comforting to Joy, and there was something in how she talked to her that seemed to communicate she understood in ways that no one Joy had met did.

"Joy," Meg said, looking at her as if she was looking into her soul, "I understand what you're going through because I had the same thing happen to me when I was in my twenties. I can remember my head being so filled with so many questions that I just wanted to curl up and wait to die."

For a moment, the numbness receded and Joy felt an intense stab of emotions. The tears began to flow.

Meg continued in an even tone. "I know when I was in your shoes, my head was filled with questions, more like screams to God about why He could let something like this happen. Unfortunately, I began to realize that God knew when I needed Him to respond to me and when I just needed to feel His presence. Now, that may sound like a load of spiritual crap, but what I experienced convinced me that God was there and present even if He wasn't going to respond to my screams. As a matter of fact, looking back on it, He seemed to be inviting me to scream at Him because only He could take those screams and redeem them into something remarkable." She paused but never took her eyes off Joy's face.

"I had a friend who explained something to me while I was in the midst of my grief that seemed pretty helpful because it allowed me to understand a little better what I was going through. She described our grief as something that is like the seasons of nature. The first season we face is a 'winter,' where we are surrounded by death and cold and numbness. During this season our biggest job, which actually comes pretty naturally, is to somehow (and this is a very individual thing) grapple with the reality of what we have lost. I have discovered that God has designed us in such a way that when we first experience a loss, our emotions seem to go into suspended animation. It's a numbness that compares with nothing we have ever felt before. Interestingly, considering the fact that we have so much to contend with during the days after someone's death, we just seem to go into robot mode and get the whole ordeal over with."

———— ⊶⊷ ————

If you're anything like Joy, it's tempting to make decisions during this time of numbness because you think that's what you need to do. These decisions can be conclusions about life, like saying, "Life isn't worth living." They can be about people and love: I'll never love again." Or they can be about God Himself: "He is cruel and distant and doesn't care about the pain I'm in." In each of these cases, we have to resist the temptation to write these conclusions in indelible ink on our heart. Why is that? The simple answer is that we hate stories that have no ending. Our automatic response is to finish the story with a conclusion like those I offered above. Stories without endings are disconcerting, unsettling, and we need to make these conclusions so that we know how the story ends. Yet these conclusions are poisonous, and they interfere with our ability to cope with the reality that confronts us. In fact, part of this season involves yearning to get out of it as soon as we can. A premature conclusion offers us that. At this point in the journey, as hard as it is, we have to commit to wrestling with the pain and emptiness we feel, and leave the end of the story to write itself rather than rushing to a conclusion.

2

WAITING TO WAKE UP

"I want to live a real life. I don't want to dream any longer."
—David in the movie *Vanilla Sky*,
written by Cameron Crowe

"Joy! It's time to get up! You can't stay in bed all day!" Joy's mom was at the bottom of the stairs and yelling up at her.

"Leave me alone, Ma!" Joy groaned. "Why can't I stay in bed all day? It's safer here," she muttered under her breath out of earshot of her mom's attentive ears. She stayed in bed a half hour longer just to make a point to anyone who would get it.

She finally dragged herself out of bed, skipped a shower, and got dressed with whatever clothes were on the floor nearest her. She didn't care what she looked like. It was an interruption just to have to be up at all. An interruption of what, though? Dreaming or reality was no more pleasant than the other.

The other complicating factor was the fact that her body had been preparing to give birth to a baby. That included her breasts preparing to feed her baby and changes to the rest of her body, including her hormones, her weight, and her emotions. It was a nightmare in the making. Dr. Miller had instructed her to wrap her chest, but it didn't help much with the discomfort of lactating without a little one to "help" her. It was one aspect of motherhood that she had heard so much about, something she was looking forward to. It felt to her that not only reality was conspiring against her, but even her body was reminding her on a daily, even hourly, basis that something had gone terribly wrong.

As she was sitting at the kitchen counter sipping on a cup of coffee (just one more reminder of Aaron being gone since she had sworn off caffeine for her pregnancy), her cell phone buzzed. She had put it on silent since Aaron's death because she didn't really want to talk to anyone, and she wanted to have the excuse that "she didn't hear it" rather than simply saying to people, "I'm really not up for talking right now." As simple as that sounds, it takes emotional energy to be diplomatic or even "nice," whatever that means, in response to others' attempt to be kind by reaching out to her.

She looked at the phone number, since she was committed to doing something with the call. It was a longtime friend, Tracy, calling. She hadn't heard from her since their high school days. She was a little surprised to hear from her, so she hit the "Decline" button and put her phone back on the counter. Her mom looked over and asked, "Who was that, Joy?"

"It was Tracy," Joy answered with a roll of her eyes. She was in no mood to talk to anyone.

"Wait, what? You mean Tracy from high school? That Tracy?" Her mom was connecting the dots.

"Yep, that Tracy." Joy was bracing herself for her mom's reaction.

"Don't you think that it's worth a shot to talk to someone other than Meg? I mean, that was a big step just to talk to anyone, and you couldn't have chosen a better person to do that with. Word has it that Tracy went through something very much like you. It might be worth a shot to hear her perspective, don't you think?" her mom offered as gently as she could.

"I don't know, Mom. I'm just not up for that. As you can see, just getting out of bed is an effort." Joy took her coffee and headed out to the deck to sit and think. It was clear that she really didn't want to be bothered.

As she sat there, she began to run through her mind some of the things Meg had said to her just a few days before. While Meg's comments were intrusive and uncomfortable, there was something about them that seemed to reflect truth to her in a way that she could accept. Something Meg said echoed in her head: "As hard as it is, you'll have to try to stay connected with people in your life." It made sense but went against everything inside her urging her to "batten down the hatches" and ride out the storm that she was trying to weather. Perhaps it was worth a shot to get out of the house and have coffee with Tracy. She was kind enough to reach out after all these years. That couldn't have been easy to do. Joy took a few more sips of her coffee and set her mind to give it a shot. It would be good to get out of the house even if it was just to take a walk.

Joy returned Tracy's call, and they decided to meet at a nearby but familiar coffee shop called Common Grounds. It was between where Tracy lived and where Joy was living. It seemed convenient and somewhat comforting since it had become a frequent haunt of Joy's since she came home from school at the state university. She would frequently go there to study, read, and occasionally journal her thoughts about what she had been learning at school.

The fateful day arrived, and Joy got up, showered, and prepared herself for her first foray into the "real world"— whatever that was—and a conversation where she had no idea how it was going to go. Tracy and Joy had been friends through high school, but when Joy decided to leave for college, they had drifted apart. Tracy had decided to go to an in-state school and, the last Joy had heard, was pursuing her degree in education. Apparently, Tracy was an aspiring elementary schoolteacher, and it fit Tracy, from what Joy remembered of her at the time. Tracy had this "presence" about her when she did her presentations in class that few other students had. She could have been selling popsicles to an Inuit but made it sound like it was the most rational and logical thing to do. She had all the requisite social and academic skills to make a great teacher.

Joy, on the other hand, went to a private school in another state. She hadn't really had a major in mind for her future. She was admitted as an undecided student, and that was the most accurate description of where she was at the time, both academically and emotionally. She hadn't been real sure where she was, but she *did* know that she wanted out of the state to break some ties that had seemed to haunt her. She had assumed that changing geographical locations would translate into emotional freedom. Now looking back, she could only wish that this had been the case. It was a hard lesson to learn that just because you change locations doesn't mean that you change the patterns of your own heart. As one of her professors would say, "The problem is that you have to take you with you!"

Common Grounds was only fifteen minutes away from her house, so Joy had some time to brace herself for what was to come, even though she had no idea what it would be. How do you prepare yourself for a conversation about something you've never experienced before? Since Aaron died, it seemed like everything in her life was changed; how she thought and even saw things was distorted and difficult to grasp. She briefly reviewed in her mind the words of Meg that were encouraging her to take this step in the first place. Everything inside her screamed to turn around and race back home to the safety of her room and her bed. In spite of that, she turned into the parking lot and parked. She wasn't real sure what she was expecting, but she walked in with as much confidence as she could muster and looked around.

Tracy had arrived ahead of her, and she waved at Joy from across the lobby. Joy brightened and made her way to the table.

"Have you already ordered, Tracy?" Joy asked.

"Yeah, I got here a half hour ago. I had some email to get through, so I thought I would just pass the time getting that out of the way while I waited for you." Tracy smiled warmly and offered Joy a hug, which Joy reciprocated.

Joy looked around and saw some familiar faces behind the bar, so she made her way to the register to place her order.

"Wow! It's been a while since I've been here." Joy was buying time, trying to figure out what she wanted to order.

"Let's go with a caramel macchiato?" she said to the barista behind the bar.

"You've got it! Coming right up!" the barista said with a tad bit too much energy and gusto. Maybe he had just had too much of what he was serving up.

"Joy!" the barista barked from behind the espresso bar.

Joy picked up her drink and walked over to the table where Tracy was still busy reading emails. She closed her laptop as Joy approached.

"First of all, I have to thank you for calling me and offering to get together. After all these years, it was a very kind gesture." Joy figured that she would get the ball rolling by recognizing Tracy's willingness to reach out.

"Not a problem at all, Joy. It seemed the least I could do considering what you're going through. When I heard that your little boy had died, I felt an immediate bond with you since I went through the same thing a few years ago." Tracy's face and tone were amazingly bright, even hopeful. Joy wondered how that was possible, but she listened attentively.

"Would you mind telling me your story, Tracy? I mean, if it isn't too difficult for you," Joy asked with care more for herself than Tracy. She wasn't convinced that she wanted to hear the story, but she knew asking was the appropriate, or kind, thing to do in this moment.

"Oh no, not at all," Tracy replied, seemingly unfazed by the prospects of telling her story again.

For Joy, if someone had asked her to share her story, she would have complied but then would be crying all the way home, having felt the pain all over again in the telling of the story. It would have felt like, just when she was beginning to get her emotional feet underneath her, the rug got pulled out again.

Tracy continued, "I had had an unfortunate 'fling'"—she put air quotes around the phrase—"that resulted in me getting pregnant. The dude left town and I never saw him again. Needless to say, I had a really tough decision to make, but in spite of the circumstances, I was convinced that the little one in my belly shouldn't have to pay for my rash decisions." Tracy paused, looking at Joy.

"Are you okay, Joy? I mean, I can stop anytime you need me to. I know how awful it feels walking out of the hospital with your arms empty." Tracy's eyes were kind and patient. Joy felt understood, even seen, but she felt a stab of pain being reminded of that day coming home from the hospital that was etched in her memory.

"Yeah, I've got to wrangle with the reality of what's happened sooner or later. I'll be okay." It took all she had within her to assert that truth. She braced for more.

Tracy nodded and picked up the rest of her story. She detailed what had happened with her little one (a little girl she named Erin) and how the doctor expressed concern about the distress her little one was displaying. It was shortly after that, that all movement ceased and she was rushed to the hospital. An emergency C-section revealed that the umbilical cord had gotten wrapped around Erin's neck, and they were unable to save her. By the time Tracy was holding her, she had died. She said something that Joy really related to. The silence was heavy and penetrating. Tracy had said her good-bye to her little one, and there was a brief memorial service a few days later. As Joy had said, it was all such a blur and felt like a bad dream that she was waiting to wake up from.

All while telling her story, Tracy seemed off in another land. She was looking out the window, down into the depths of her coffee cup, and seemingly beyond Joy. Joy knew that feeling of being separated from your feelings for sure, even though Tracy seemed completely unaware of them. Suddenly, a thought began to form in Joy's mind. How could Tracy seem so composed and detached from her story? What was going on?

Tracy looked at Joy with clarity in her eyes and said, " That was three years, seven, months and two days ago."

Joy was puzzled. She asked, "Tracy, how can you tell your story with such detail and almost no emotion? How do you that?"

Tracy looked surprised as if the answer was obvious. "While I know that it all happened—I mean, I have an empty bassinet in the extra room in my apartment—there are two things I've discovered to get through it all."

She paused, and what she said next reminded Joy of a news anchor on the cable news networks. "Quite honestly, I'm just waiting for it all to be over. I've managed to accept the reality of what has happened, but I refuse to accept what it means for my future, or what it means about me and my life.

As long as I can stay in this waiting mode, I can manage most anything. So, the first thing I've done is committed myself to living in a 'wait and see' mode. I've never told anyone this, but quite honestly I'm waiting to be told that Erin actually survived and was adopted by a family, and that I can go see her again. I know that sounds a little crazy, but it makes living with this horror a little easier."

Tracy again paused and looked out the window again as the cars rolled by waiting for their turn at the drive-through window of the coffee shop.

"The other thing I discovered is that I can take all the memories, and all the feelings, and all the thoughts I have about Erin and put them in a lockbox in my head. They are safely contained there and can't interfere with the life I now lead so I can keep going. Occasionally, I go back and open the box up again, but not for very long. It's all self-pity anyway." Tracy locked eyes with Joy, seemingly just for emphasis.

"So, that's my story, Joy." Tracy sighed and settled back in her chair. "I hope it's encouraging to you, and I want you to know that if you ever need someone to vent your emotions or thoughts to, just text me. I'll be happy to get a cup of coffee again."

Joy had to get out of there as quickly as she could. She found herself having a hard time breathing and connecting any thoughts at all. It seemed like she had just been ushered into an alternate universe and was now suffering jet lag coming back to her own reality. She thanked Tracy for taking the time to meet with her, and she would take her up on her invitation. As she got in her car, the tears began to flow again. It wasn't wracking sobs like it'd been in the past, but just a steady flow down her cheeks. She said to herself and no one in particular as she was driving, "I'll never do that again."

The biggest difference between Tracy and Joy is their level of acceptance of the feelings they were experiencing. Tracy had landed on an approach to control and contain these emotions, then added a justification for it by saying, "I've accepted the reality." Instead, all she had done was accept the *facts,* but she hadn't accepted the meaning of what had happened to her. Joy, on the other hand, made a quick comparison to Tracy and concluded that there was something wrong with her. In terms of emotions, she was leaking out everywhere and assumed that that indicated she was doing her grief all wrong.

Perhaps you are feeling a lot like Tracy. You are just waiting for this nightmare to be over. So you have landed on a strategy to just make do with life as you have it, not investing in anything that would provoke feelings that unbalance your tenuous hold on reality. Additionally, as time progresses through the winter of your grief, you have had more and more time to construct a system of thoughts and conclusions that imprison all these feelings and memories. We often resort to using shame as a method of quelling the rebellion of our feelings and thoughts that seemingly want to overthrow our iron-fisted control over them. This shame strategy shows itself through something that Tracy said to Joy: "It's all self-pity anyway." We often will gladly sacrifice our own self-care in service to control and containment.

Your challenge today is finding ways to be gentle with yourself instead of comparing yourself to someone else. If you have something that would feel comforting, like listening to your favorite music, or taking a bath or shower, or taking a long walk, give yourself permission to do that today. You would never treat someone with the kind of pain you are experiencing with insensitivity. When Jesus said, "Love your neighbor *as yourself,*" He laid the foundation for our gentleness, compassion, and grace for others, and that foundation includes practicing the same for ourselves.

3

WHY CAN'T I FEEL ANYTHING?

"Numb the dark and you numb the light."
—Brené Brown

Joy found herself trying to recover from her conversation with Tracy. While she had managed to find someone to talk to who had a clue about what life was like losing a little one, this conversation was far from comforting. She was reflecting on two thoughts at the same time. They seemed to be in a wrestling match with each other. One thought was her recollection from talking to Meg and being told to lean into people in her life who could allow her to process her feelings and thoughts about what she was going through. She thought she was doing that by getting coffee with Tracy, but it sure didn't turn out the way Meg had made it sound.

The other thought was more of a question: *Is Tracy onto something in approaching her grief in that way?* She sure seemed confident in her approach to handling her grief that way, but something just didn't feel right to Joy. Something was missing, and she couldn't put her finger on it. As a matter of fact, Joy had this sense that she wasn't so sure she wanted to nail it down. It might mean she was doing something wrong . . . whatever that was.

She was sitting on her bed and looked across her room, which seemed to be the safest place on earth right now, and caught sight of the notebook Meg had brought with her. She said that she was going to leave it for her, but Joy didn't even want to get near it for fear of all the emotions that would be provoked.

"Nope, I ain't doing it. I don't care what Meg encouraged me to do, I'm not doing it." She spoke out loud to no one in particular, but it felt more solid to say it aloud. She still wasn't sure how she was going to sort out these thoughts she was having, but something else had been weighing on her lately: she felt nothing.

Joy walked over and picked up the notebook and headed to the back deck. She put it down on a side table next to a chaise lounger as if it were radioactive; then she went back into the kitchen to make herself a cup of tea. It was later in the day, and tea seemed like a good choice to calm her unsettledness around making some of these feelings, or lack thereof, real.

I really don't know where to start with this journal. Meg told me that I should take some time to communicate my thoughts somewhere so I could see them and make them real, but I'm not convinced, given my conversation with Tracy, if that is such a good idea. It annoys me that I'm doing this at all. I mean, why does this have to be so hard?? Aaron wasn't even alive when he was born! I didn't even get to meet him and see his personality or anything. I think the thing that is so irritating is that I feel nothing at all. You would think that with something this big happening in a person's life, Tracy would be devastated and inconsolable. I mean, nothing anyone could say or do would make it any better, right? How can you make something better that isn't there? I look at the "reality" of what has happened, and it feels like a "whiteout" in my head and emotions.

Joy's thoughts trailed back into her history with her family. Many years ago, they had traveled to the mountains to spend some time on the slopes and just hang out as a family. As she thought about it, a faint smile formed on her lips. She would never forget, when they were about a half hour away from the ski resort, they hit a literal whiteout of snow and wind. Her dad was driving, and her mom looked tense and uncertain.

Thinking back on that trip, she now felt like she had been feeling looking out the window of their car, except this was looking into the window of her own soul. She couldn't see anything in spite of the fact that clearly there was a lot going on.

I guess this whiteout is more a matter of too much going on in my head and heart than what I can possibly track. There have been times where I have just given up and was just existing—like Tracy has been doing. Just waiting for the nightmare to be over. Yet with each passing day there is a little bit more.

There is something else that really bothers me. WHAT IS WRONG WITH ME??? My own son has died, and I don't feel anything! Really? Something must be dramatically wrong that I can't seem to even generate some amount of sadness about it. Everything is just numb. That's my biggest concern today. I'm just not feeling anything, like I'm walking through my days in a completely emotionless state.

I remember that book my psychology prof had me read about pain, and now it all is starting to make sense. My emotional nerves have been seared and are in a numb state. Of course, knowing that isn't all that helpful or hopeful because sooner or later they have to wake up, right? So what do I do with all this?? Nothing? Isn't there some solution to be applied here so that my feelings come back? No, wait . . . what am I saying? Do I really want my feelings back? Unfortunately, my feelings are connected with Aaron, and clearly when he died, something in me died. I wish I knew what to do. Ugh, enough. I'm done for today.

In many respects, Joy is right. Something *was* dramatically wrong. Her little boy died, and she was in a very natural state of numbness after such an immense loss. It's interesting how easily we can overlook the obvious. Our grief, particularly in times like these, seems at once familiar and invisible in spite of how much of it dominates our emotional landscape. It is a fundamental characteristic of being human.

Why is it so hard to embrace or accept our own humanity? Put simply, it is hard to embrace because it means that we have to grapple with our vulnerability and loss of control. In everyday life we are not frequently confronted with these aspects of being human. As a matter of fact, we do everything we can to minimize our risk of being exposed and feeling profoundly out of control. There is no one single event that reminds us more of our vulnerability and lack of control than death. It is the defining aspect of our existence that reminds us just how vulnerable to hurt and pain we are, as well as our true lack of control. Being human means having relationships, and when those end, we feel pain. With a loss of this magnitude, however—though we shouldn't compare one loss to another—it is a tidal wave of emotions, thoughts, and feelings to such a degree that there seems to be nothing left behind. We are left reeling from the impact of such an emotional tsunami that in some respects the numbness is a mercy. It provides us with the emotional breathing room we need to survey and landscape, and then begin the journey of recovery.

There is one more aspect of this discussion of processing our thoughts and feelings while we are in the throes of our denial. The overriding motivation of denial is to control and contain the pain we are experiencing. Our major task during this season of our grief is the acceptance of the reality in which we are living. Because it is so big, so overwhelming, so all-encompassing, we will seek whatever means possible to control the overwhelming power of the reality we are facing. One of the primary strategies we often use is comparison. As a matter of fact, you will see in her interactions with Tracy that Joy was busy comparing her experiences with Tracy's. When we are in a place that we don't recognize or know, specifically when we experience the death of someone we love, our innate tendency as humans is to look for a reference point. This reference—the other person—exists so we can judge "where we are," either in an emotional universe or even in the physical world. We are all committed comparers, particularly when it comes to our emotions, and that usually leads us to conclude that we are doing something "wrong" because, of course, what the other person is doing is the "right" way. Why do we do that? We do it to re-establish our sense of control and diminish our sense of weakness and vulnerability. What we don't realize is that looking around for a comparison point only heightens the pain we feel. Not only have we suffered a devastating loss, but we are also experiencing a diminishment of our social standing because we can't handle this immense emotional load of loss, which is humiliating and just plain embarrassing.

One thing to realize is that during each season of our grief there are a variety of tools we can use. Needless to say, Joy leaned in on one of the key tools during the winter of our grief, and that is journaling. The whole idea of journaling may be daunting to you since most of us fall into a comparison loop about our writing (compared to whom, Hemingway?). It's important to recognize that your journaling is for you. No one else. If it matches what is going on in your head and heart, then you've accomplished what you set out to do. In his popular play *Macbeth*, Shakespeare's main character says, "Don't keep your grief inside. Speak your sorrow. Grief that is not expressed will whisper in your heart until it breaks." The key to recognize what he says in the second half of the quote: "Grief that is not expressed will whisper in your heart until it breaks"[2] There is something to be said for giving our grief words. Of course, the challenge in giving our grief words is that it makes them real. Yes, while this would appear to be a disadvantage of articulating what we are experiencing, but it is also a validation. During this stop on our journey, take some time to write down the challenges you've faced with the emotions and thoughts you have had today.

4

SAFE PEOPLE

*"Courage gives us a voice and compassion gives us
an ear. Without both, there is no opportunity for empathy
and connection."*

—Brené Brown

"Do you really think that is such a good idea, Joy?" Her mom had a concerned look on her face. It was clear she was questioning Joy's judgment about going back to the cemetery.

"I don't know, Mom. There is just too much of this that just doesn't feel real, and I feel a real draw to retrace my steps just to assure myself that it is. You can be sure that I really don't want to but—"

"Then why do it?" Joy's mom cut her off, adding, "It just seems so soon after Aaron's passing to do something like that." She sighed with her own grief bubbling to the surface.

Joy's anger flared at the euphemism her mom was using about Aaron's death. It just seemed to cheapen and minimize the gravity of what had happened. "He *died*, Mom! He didn't just pass away. He *died*!"

"Okay, okay, you're right. It's okay. My apologies for not choosing the 'right' words to describe what happened, Joy." Joy's mom was taken aback by the intensity of Joy's anger. She wasn't a person to flare with anger like that. But she kept quiet and let the silence settle in between them.

"I'm sorry, Mom, I don't know why I jumped on you like that. I'm just tired of the way people talk about my little boy with their idiotic euphemisms as if doing so will ease the pain. Nothing will ease the pain, nothing . . ." Her voiced trailed off as she once again became lost in thought in the events of the last few weeks.

Joy quickly prepared a cup of tea and walked out to the deck to sit and think, doing everything she could not to let her emotions get the best of her. As she sat, she reviewed what had motivated her to want to go to the cemetery. As she said to her mom, nothing seemed real to her. The ache and pain she felt was very real, and it had become a constant, unwanted companion through her days following the memorial service. Everything was upside down; at least that's how it felt.

Her thoughts drifted back to her days in college. She had decided to pursue a major in psychology since of all the various courses she had taken during her freshman year, this was the only area of study that seemed to capture her interest because of its applicability across all of her life. At one point in her academic career, she seriously considered pursuing a master's degree in counseling because of her heart for people and the pain they experience in life. At that time, she felt compassion for them. Now she was beginning to realize that God had bigger plans for her pursuing of that subject area. It was to prepare her for what was to come. Of course, she had been warned during one of her classes, a class on grief and loss, that there was no way to prepare for the pain one feels when grieving. Holy cow was that spot on.

She recalled the prof talking about how grief was a lot like a burn wound, except a psychological and emotional one. She suddenly realized that Meg had used a very similar word picture to describe the numbness she was feeling. Anyway, he painted a pretty horrifying picture of how extreme burn wounds used to be treated by doctors in the past. He described that they would plunge the burn victims into a whirlpool, give them a shot of a high-powered pain medication, and then scrub their wounds. Even in spite of the pain meds, they would still cry out. His point was that without scrubbing their wounds, they would die. The scabs that formed overnight would become an incubator for bacteria that would kill the patient. Therefore, they had to keep the wounds clean and appropriately medicated in order for healing to occur. The connection he made to the grieving process was that often the work of grieving involves "scrubbing the wound." It hurts like no other, but that is the only way that healing will be achieved. She realized that her draw to the cemetery might be her attempt not only to remind herself of the reality that happened but also to allow herself to feel the wound again.

"Ugh, that sounds horrible!" she said out loud to no one in particular. She didn't want to go. At the same time, she still felt that she needed to visit her son's grave for herself, so she called her friend Phoebe and proposed going.

Phoebe and Joy had become good friends at college and shared a number of classes together. After Joy's disastrous interaction with Tracy, she wasn't so keen on letting anyone else into her life other than maybe her family. She remembered what she had said after it was all over—that she wouldn't do that again. On the other hand, she had been reflecting on *exactly* what Meg had said about leaning on people in her life, and she realized that she had managed to leave out an important description that Meg had given her about those people. Meg had said, "Important, safe, and trustworthy people." The way Meg had said it with such specificity and purpose, Joy wasn't sure what she had meant. It was something Joy made a mental note to ask Meg about when they were together again, whenever that would be.

In the meantime, Joy was pretty sure that Phoebe would probably fit into one of those categories. Phoebe had been through her fair share of pain and grief in her own life, and interestingly enough, it hadn't made her bitter or even cynical. Phoebe wasn't prone to put up with euphemisms and platitudes. As a matter of fact, Joy remembered that Phoebe got really frustrated when such platitudes would be served up to hurting people she was around. After a specific interaction involving mutual friends, they were sitting at the coffee shop on campus and talking about a conversation among their friends. Phoebe was visibly upset about how their friend had been treated. Finally, after blowing off some emotional steam, Phoebe retorted, "People have no idea how damaging those platitudes are. It seems to me that they are more concerned with appearing profound than taking the time to be present with someone in pain." Joy was stunned by such a powerful statement about caring for people, and her respect for Phoebe only grew more that day. Joy was still fascinated by that and wanted to know more about it, but when they graduated, they went their own ways. They managed to keep in touch occasionally through the social media platforms they were both on, but not much more than that.

———— ◦◦◦ ————

Probably one of the most difficult tasks during our grief is to find "safe" people to be a part of our social network. The reality is that we have a wide variety of people in our everyday lives, but not all are "safe." Of course, the adjective "safe" is flexibly defined according to the person you talk to, but there are some constants to keep in mind. Most people would say that someone is safe if they can keep a confidence and are consistently supportive during our tough times. While that is indeed important, the bigger issue isn't characteristics as much as it is our ability to evaluate the people who enter our lives. A good example is from the difference between Phoebe and Tracy, each of whom had a very different impact on Joy's life. While Joy had just resigned herself to wait out life until it changed, Phoebe was the kind of person who was clearly motivated by her empathy for others rather than controlling the experiences and emotions of her friends. She was strongly motivated to enter into Joy's sorrow and, by her presence or well-timed words, validate Joy's experience and emotions. By doing so, she created a space for Joy to accept her own emotions because she was safe in her relationship with Phoebe. Tracy, on the other hand, was so buttoned up that there wasn't anything to respond to. In some ways, she was buttoned up, and she expected other people to do the same. The name of the game for Tracy was to control and suppress whatever emotions she had with the express purpose of remaining functional and doing whatever she could to avoid her own drama. What it reduces down to are the difference between connection (Phoebe) and control (Tracy).

What is important to take note of here is that Joy's description of her relationship or memories of Phoebe were great observations of Phoebe's character and "safeness." This kind of analysis is exactly what we have to do during the toughest time of our lives, which illustrates an important point. We need to be developing the skill of seeing character in people way before we suffer a significant loss. That may not match where you are today, and that's okay. You may have to rely on key people in your life to help you evaluate the people you're spending time with, just like Joy's mother was attempting to do. Who are the safe people in your life—not because you like them but because they have demonstrated empathy and compassion for the state of your heart?

5

SEARCHING FOR
THE PLAYBOOK

*"Of course there is no formula for success, except perhaps an
unconditional acceptance of life, and what it brings."*
—Arthur Rubenstein

A new day dawned for Joy, and she woke up feeling hopeful and not quite as heavy as she had so many days before. It had been a few weeks since the conversation with Meg, and she had been mulling over what Meg had told her about Aaron's room. She had encouraged Joy to go back into the room and experience it fully. As she had walked by the room many times throughout the course of the last few weeks, she had cast a brief glance in to see just how true it had been that she had mummified the room. One day, she even stood in the doorway and turned on the light in the room just to survey it once again. It didn't seem quite as onerous as it had been on the day she had accidentally walked fully into the room and melted down in a flood of memories. As she stood there looking, she worked to give herself permission not to be ready just yet to tackle the room, or his baby clothes, or even remotely ready to think about changing the room at all. For whatever reason, his room was the only thing that reminded her of Aaron, but over the course of the next few days, she found out just how wrong she had been.

Joy thought that she felt good enough to venture out by herself. She figured that she could use the distraction of going window shopping. It seemed harmless enough, and even though she wasn't going to buy anything, walking around a mall that had a variety of shops and a wonderful food court seemed to be a good way to spend her morning. Besides, she had a visit with a friend who was going to meet her for lunch at a restaurant near the mall, so this fit right into the flow of her activities for the day.

Alyssa was a friend from her college days. She was a junior as Joy was entering school as a freshman. Alyssa was her RA in the dorm Joy was living in, and Joy loved her. She was kind and funny and had a perceptiveness that reminded her a lot of Meg, but a much younger version. They struck up a wonderful friendship during Alyssa's senior year and would often spend a Friday night together with other friends watching old reruns of *The Office* on Netflix. As it turned out, after graduating, Alyssa fell in love and married a guy from another university just one town over. She got pregnant, and like Joy, when she went into labor, there were complications and their little one died shortly after birth. Her husband seemed to change dramatically after that and drifted away from Alyssa. He got romantically involved with someone at his work, and Alyssa found out. Unfortunately, in spite of Alyssa's best efforts with counseling and hopes for reconciliation, Michael, her husband, wasn't interested and initiated divorce proceedings. In a matter of a year and a half, Alyssa was grieving not only the loss of her baby but also the disintegration of her marriage.

Needless to say, Alyssa was no stranger to grief and loss. After hearing what Joy had been through, she reached out to get together. Joy put her off time and time again, but Alyssa was patient and would check in with her every other week or so, and eventually Joy relented and accepted the invitation to have lunch. That day was going to be today, and Joy had strongly mixed feelings about it. While it seemed like one more step into the reality she was *supposed* to accept, Joy was still unsure that she had the strength or even the motivation to move further into this season of grief. In spite of all that, she thought it might be well timed given the conversation she had had with Meg, so she did all she could do to keep a positive attitude about it. At least she would have the distraction of a shopping trip before that.

Joy stopped by the last store and meandered over to the restaurant that she and Alyssa had agreed upon. Thankfully, it was a quiet place to meet rather than a noisy "fast-casual" place that populates many malls these days. She checked in with the hostess to see if Alyssa had been seated yet. The hostess's face brightened as she mentioned her name, and she turned and headed into the restaurant saying over her shoulder, "Yes, she's here. Let me show you to the table."

"Joy! It's so good to see you!!" Alyssa saw her coming and slid out of the booth and gave her a warm hug. "I've been looking forward to this since we talked," she said.

"Hi, Alyssa! Wow! It's been a while, hasn't it? I'm so sorry I haven't stayed in touch better," Joy responded.

"Oh, don't worry about it. Life happens, right?" Alyssa replied, smiling.

"Yeah, if that's what you want to call it," Joy responded to Alyssa, trying to gauge if there was more to Alyssa's comment than just what she said. After her conversation with Tracy, Joy was on high alert for such details.

"I guess it depends on how we define 'life' right? Or, something else intrudes into our life and interferes with our best-laid plans." Alyssa's expression turned serious but filled with compassion. "I'm so sorry to hear what happened to your little one, Joy. That must have been awful."

"Yeah, awful would be a tame description of how my life has been since we had the memorial service and all the dust settled. It seems like everyone and their lives go on, and I feel frozen in time with all my emotions, memories, and thoughts." Joy accepted a glass of water from the server and took a sip of the water just to fill the space after what she had said.

"I can't say that I don't know what that's like," Alyssa responded, nodding. "I can vividly remember many times in the first few months after Emma died—that's what we named her before she was born—that it felt like I was living in suspended animation. My feelings seemed to match the weather outside since it was winter. Everything was frozen inside me, and looking back now, I think I would say that there was God's mercy in that since I was nowhere ready to process what was going on in my heart.

"There's one thing that I would want to convey to you given the place you're at. Be very, very careful not to fall into making comparisons about your journey through grief with anyone else's. I did that, and it stole the opportunity I had to validate the feelings I was experiencing and the memories and thoughts I was wrestling with. You will find that there will be plenty of people who want to pontificate about how to grieve who have either never experienced it or who have done nothing but deny and minimize it. They tend to think that their way is the *best* way."

"Wow! That's exactly what I've been feeling lately. It seems like no matter how I feel or what I do, it feels like I'm not doing anything right," Joy replied.

"Yes, exactly, Joy! I have learned from hard experience that when I was sunken in the swamp of emotions during my grief, I was looking for anything to tell me how to do grief. Therefore, when people would describe their experiences, I would make the comparison to my own, trying to figure out a way to replicate what they were doing. Unfortunately, I was using their experiences as the standard for my experiences, and that is horribly unfair to *my* experiences. It's almost as if what I was going through wasn't nearly as important as what they were going through, and so I just needed to copy them."

At that moment, Joy felt like she was talking to someone who "got it." It was comforting to know that she was not alone in how she was feeling.

Alyssa continued, "We are always looking for a formula or a playbook by which to manage our pain and our grief. It's pretty natural for us to do that. We seem to strive to make our uncertainty about walking this process more certain, and that way we can feel less vulnerable."

So often during this journey of grief, particularly during the winter of our grief, we are searching for clues and signs that would indicate we are "doing it right." Unfortuantely, this search for the "right" way interferes with our ability to experience our own feelings, thoughts, and conclusions. That connects with what Alyssa said at the end of her conversation with Joy. We want not only to know how the journey will end, but we want a play-by-play description that will allow us to relax and engage in the process. The problem is that grief is never that neat and clean. Annoyingly, it is messy, confusing, and impossibly frustrating. For most people, this journey is one that they have never taken before, and they are searching for anything that will tell them, or even more so assure them, that it will all work out, whatever that means. The challenge of the journey through our grief is that it invites us to trust—trust other people and trust God in the midst of it all. Our demands for certainty and clarity are our way of avoiding trusting anyone. We are searching for some firm ground to stand on other than the tsunami of emotions and thoughts we have. While that is understandable, what we are more in need of are traveling companions who understand this journey rather than an absolute certainty of the path ahead.

6

TIME HEALS ALL WOUNDS

"I've learned . . . that love, not time, heals all wounds."
—Andy Rooney

B en's cell phone rang on the kitchen counter where he had left it. He was out on the deck of his university dorm room, "Hey, Tom! Can you get that?"

"Sure," Tom yelled back. "Hello? Hi, Mr. Andrews. Yeah, Ben is here, do you want to talk to him? Sure, here he is."

By that time, Ben was already coming back in to take a phone call that was obviously for him.

"Hey, Dad! How's it going?" Ben was already suspicious; his dad's voice was shaky and quiet. He wasn't his usual ebullient self.

"Ben, I've got some bad news. Your mom collapsed a few days ago, and we thought it was no big deal. Her cancer, as far as we knew, was in remission and there was no threat. So, we went to the hospital as a precaution. But once we got there and they did all their tests, the doctor told us that her cancer is back and advancing so fast that it has already invaded her internal organs. Ben, they aren't giving her very much time. You need to get home as quickly as you can."

"Absolutely, Dad, I'll leave within the hour." Ben had a sick feeling that what was going to happen in the next few days was going to be all that they had feared was going to happen eventually. It was all he could do to rein in the wild horses of catastrophe and death running him over. When he had left for school that fall, he thought that he had accepted the reality of his mom's impending death, but given what he was feeling, he began to doubt whether he had really accepted it at all.

Over the next few days, his mom steadily deteriorated. They moved her to hospice care within the week, and the feared day finally came. Ben, his sister, Christine, and their dad stood around their mom's bed while she struggled to breathe. They prayed, they sang, and they reminisced about old times. Occasionally, his mom would smile as they laughed over old times. Eventually, her breathing slowed and then finally stopped. They all looked numbly at each other, and each began to cry. The nurses rushed in, surveyed the situation, and quietly exited the room. They gathered around each other hugging, hanging on for dear life. They each went to the bed and said good-bye, kissing her for a final time. Ben and his sister left the room while his dad took his final moments with his wife. Ben and Christine could hear the muffled cries and moans coming from the room. How were they going to survive without the glue that their mom seemed to provide the family? What was going to happen to each of them as they tried to make sense of something so senseless.

Ben went back to school two weeks later, and he threw himself into his studies in the coming weeks. School was a welcome distraction from the pool of pain he had been swimming through over the last month or so. Amazingly enough, he made it through finals and his final projects. He was quite shocked that he actually pulled it off. He was feeling pretty anxious about going back home. His sister was a senior in high school, and as he'd talked to her over the last few weeks, he realized that she was sinking into a dark depression. His dad wasn't much better, but because he had the responsibility to try to keep the family together, he seemed to be doing better than anyone. Ben didn't get it, but he was thankful that there was one less person he had to worry about.

When Ben got home, he dove into spending time with his sister, whatever he could do to help her talk about their mom and her feelings. They would go out and watch the latest movie or take off for the mountains to do some skiing, which they hadn't done since their mom had been sick. While his sister was talking about their mom, Ben noticed that he felt absolutely nothing. He was relieved to a certain extent, but he knew that he not only had lost his mom but also seemed to be losing his memories of her.

One evening when he was sitting with his dad by the fireplace and sipping a soda, he began to tell his dad about his concerns about his memories.

"How long has this been going on, Ben?" his dad asked.

"Oh, probably since I went back to school. I wasn't really paying attention to it actually. All I was really worried about was getting through school and trying to keep my grades up . . . " His voice trailed off as he was beginning to realize that the memories had been gone far longer than he had assumed.

"I certainly get that," his dad replied. "I did the same thing with work for a while, but I had the advantage, if you can call it that, of sleeping in an empty bed to remind me of what I was doing to try not to feel so bad, which is an understatement. I began to realize that if I was going to bury my grief and feelings over your mom being gone, I was going to lose other things as well—namely, my memories. They're kind of a package deal unfortunately."

"I guess I never thought of it that way, but what about 'time heals all wounds'?" Ben was fighting getting overwhelmed by the emotions he was beginning to feel.

"Time doesn't heal all wounds, Ben. Participating in life is the way that we heal from things like losing your mother.

Waiting for wounds to heal is only wasting time and leaving it to circumstances to heal us. The last I checked, circumstances usually don't help me because they are out of my control. I don't like feeling like a victim to my emotions and how I respond to your mother's death. My healing, my recovery, is my responsibility and no one else's."

It was almost as if his dad was reminding himself of something he had forgotten.

It is easy to fall into the trap of thinking that time heals all wounds. It is a trite phrase that people say particularly around losses of any significance. "Just give it some time," or, "You just need some time, and things will look a little better." While their attempts to comfort and encourage are commendable, they are misplaced and often set up the expectation that grieving is nothing more than waiting for life to change and get better. It is little wonder that therapists who work in this area of grief and grieving often refer to it as "grief work." That's exactly what it is. It is focusing on allowing our grief to exist and to feel the weight of the loss we have experienced, which means accepting the realities that confront us when we've lost someone.

Finally, remember that accepting the reality isn't only a matter of assenting to the facts of what happened. It means embracing all that it means to us regarding the person we have lost.

7

I Can't Remember Anything!

"Only people who are capable of loving strongly can also suffer great sorrow, but this same necessity of loving serves to counteract their grief and heals them."
—Leo Tolstoy

"Ben, you know that I've been going to my men's group for a long time, right?"

"Yeah, I've known that for years, Dad. What of it?" Ben was suspicious where this was going.

"Well, the one thing that many of them told me was that I needed to connect with a counselor to talk about losing your mom." Ben's dad looked at him steadily.

He continued, "I've been going for about four weeks now, and it has been really helpful . . . more than I expected it to be." He paused.

"What worries me, Ben, is that you haven't had any time at all to process what you've been feeling since your mother died. I want you to do the same thing. I want you go with me next time. It's coming up in a couple of days."

"You've got to be kidding me, Dad! There is no way that I'm talking to someone about how I'm feeling. What can he do? Can he bring Mom back? No! What's he going to say to me? Is he going to tell me that I just need to express my feelings and everything is going to be okay? Nothing is going to be okay, Dad! Nothing, hear me? I will forever be without my mom!" The tears had begun to flow, and that made Ben even angrier. "She isn't going to be there when I get married or Christine gets married! She isn't going to be there to hold her grandbabies. There is no way that this hole in my heart will ever heal, and no one is going to help me with that! No! I'm not going, I don't care if this guy is Jesus Christ himself!"

His dad was quiet and was watching him steadily as he ranted for that moment in time. He couldn't contain his emotions. He was shaking. He grabbed his coat, stormed out the door, and slammed it behind him.

He took a walk around the block and stopped off at a park bench where he and his mom would often stop and sit to talk about life. He sat there transfixed by a frantic search for the memories of his mom. He couldn't come up with any. That made him even more frightened and angry. He launched off the park bench like it was made of molten metal and he had gotten burned. As he walked, he began to slow down emotionally, and his gait slowed from a fast-paced power walk to a stroll.

When he got home, his dad was waiting in the living room. He was reading and took off his glasses as Ben came in the door. Ben looked at his dad, and quietly said, "I'll go once, Dad . . . for you. I don't expect anything good to come of it, but I'll go because you want me to, not because I want to go."

His dad looked at him with a look of intense compassion intermixed with his own pain. "I'll take that, Ben. The appointment is at two on Thursday."

That Thursday came, and Ben woke up that morning with a sense of dread. It felt a little like he was going through all the emotions he'd been working so hard to keep under wraps. He drug himself out of bed and stumbled to the kitchen to get a cup of coffee. His dad left a note for him on the counter: "Had to take the car in for a maintenance check . . . back in a couple of hours." Ben was thankful to be alone with his thoughts, so he wandered out to the deck, pulled a chair over, and sat down to survey the back lawn and the mountains in the distance. He always loved sitting out here to think and just be.

Before long, his thoughts turned to the upcoming counseling appointment with his dad. He didn't know much about this counselor, but he was willing to humor his dad since he was feeling so bad too. As he sat there, he thought back to the various interactions with counselors that he'd had in the past. Actually he'd never had any direct interaction with a counselor; he'd only learned about them from his friends who had gone to the university counseling center where he went to school. He always would listen and think, *I'm glad I don't have to go to one of those!* He never admitted it, but he assumed that counselors were only for people who were really screwed up and had run to the end of their rope in handling life. Going with his dad felt like an indictment of his ability to cope with life.

"Ben, I'm home!" His dad yelled from the kitchen. "We probably need to get ready to head over to the counselor's office. I don't want to be late." His dad stuck his head out the deck door and smiled at him.

"Okay, Dad. How long is it going to take to get there?" Ben asked, hoping it wouldn't be a long car ride.

"Oh, probably fifteen to twenty minutes," his dad answered.

"All right, let me finish my coffee and I'll be in," Ben replied.

Well, here we go, he thought to himself. *I said I would go, so I'm going to have to follow through.* He got up and walked into the kitchen looking for his shoes, found them, and went in search of his dad.

He found him in his study typing furiously on the keyboard and looking at the screen with an irritated look on his face.

"Everything all right, dad?"

"Yeah, yeah, everything is fine. It's just funny to me that companies give employees plenty of sick time, but when it comes to bereavement time, it's as if we are supposed to get over it in a week and get on with life," his dad said, shaking his head.

"Well, it's time to go. You set? Let's head out." His dad shot a glance over to him, and he nodded.

Once they got in the car and headed down the highway to the office, Ben asked his dad, "So, who is this counselor, Dad? And how did you find him . . . or her?"

"It's a him, Ben. I got a referral from a friend of mine in the men's group from church. He seems like a good guy and makes it pretty easy to talk about this stuff. His name is Dr. Greg Wheatley. I think you might like him if you give him a chance." He looked expectantly at Ben.

The office was nothing like Ben had expected. Of course, he hadn't taken any time to think through what he expected. He immediately realized that he had some very distorted views of counselors and what a counseling office looks like. He and his dad walked up to the receptionist at the front desk and checked in. The receptionist smiled and said, "Dr. Wheatley will be with you in a few minutes. He's just finishing up with the appointment before you."

Dr. Wheatley came to the door of the reception area and greeted Ben's dad warmly with a handshake. He extended his hand to shake Ben's as well. "Hey Ben! It's good to finally meet you. Your dad's been telling me so much about you!

Let's head back to my office." He turned and walked down a hallway punctuated by office doors with slotted windows in each. As Ben walked by each door, he saw a counselor already seated and talking to his or her client. His unsettledness seemed to subside as they walked further toward Dr. Wheatley's office.

"Ah, here we are!" Dr. Wheatley said. "Just make yourself comfortable wherever." As Ben walked into the moderately sized office, it seemed that his heart rate slowed considerably. All he could think over and over again was, *This isn't what I expected at all!*

Ben took in the office in a swift glance. There were diplomas on the wall over a desk strewn with a variety of papers, folders, and sticky notes. As he continued to survey the office, he noticed a small tabletop running water fountain, which gave the office an atmosphere of a spa instead of a counselor's office. There was a loveseat against one wall and a couple of overstuffed chairs facing each other at opposite ends of a coffee table. Ben made a beeline for the overstuffed chair as far away from what he guessed was the counselor's chair opposite him. His dad seemed to have a favorite spot on the loveseat and settled in next to Ben.

Ben is typical of young men who suffer grief. Ben has more than enough tasks and activities to distract him from the pain he is experiencing. Ben is displaying the fight that occurs when we try to control and contain the pain that threatens to overwhelm us by the loss of someone we love. One of the key losses in addition to the person who has died is often the memories we have of them. While they are the very things that we fear losing the most, when we land on the control-and-contain strategy, we are choosing to avoid the feelings that those memories bring with them. Therefore, it's a little like a circuit breaker in your home. You shut down one panel of circuits, you shut down all the devices, lamps, and everything in those rooms connected to it. This is the "room" of our hearts that has the feelings that make the memories what they are. We certainly can choose to "not feel," but unfortunately the memories go with the feelings. This is simply one more strategy that we are searching for that will bring some relief during this winter of our grief. That is what King David was referring to below when he said, "All day long I go about mourning":

I am bowed down and brought very low;
all day long I go about mourning.
My back is filled with searing pain;
there is no health in my body.
I am feeble and utterly crushed;
I groan in anguish of heart. (Psalm 38:6–8 NIV)

8

A Prison of My Own Making

"Walled in by desires, fears frozen inside my self-built prison the whirling world passes before my hooded eyes."

—Socalalto

"So, Bob," Dr. Wheatley said, looking at Ben's dad, "I see that you have brought your son along. It's good to finally meet you, Ben! You seem to be a bright spot these days for your dad as he wades through the aftermath of your mom's death."

Ben cringed at the word death. It just seemed so harsh and cruel, and yet it was descriptive. He realized that he had grown comfortable with the euphemisms people had been using with him and his family like "passed away" or "losing your mom."

"Yeah, I told him I'd come in this one time for him. I honestly don't really see the point in telling a complete stranger your problems. Not to mention the fact that it doesn't bring my mom back. Sorry, but I thought I would get all the cards on the table before we get much further." Ben could feel the frustration begin to rise, just as it did when he and his dad talked about the whole counseling thing the first time.

"Fair enough, Ben. Thanks for your honesty and forthrightness. I really do appreciate it. It's not often that I have clients come into my office and do such a thing as you just did. I'm beginning to see why your dad is so proud of you. Do you mind if I ask you a few questions based on what you just said?" Dr. Wheatley paused to see Ben's response.

"Let 'er rip, doc! You're the one driving the bus here. I'm just along for the ride." Ben smiled, thinking that he had effectively neutralized the threat the counselor represented to his fragile hold on his emotions.

"Interesting turn of phrase, Ben." Dr. Wheatley cocked his head as if to consider what was fully meant by the hasty wall Ben was erecting to keep himself safe from all intruders.

"So, let me ask you this, Ben. What happens when you think about yourself and your relationship with your mom?" Dr. Wheatley was following the typical counselor path, as far as Ben could tell.

"I don't feel much of anything." At that moment, Ben felt the draw of Dr. Wheatley's gaze and something welling up inside him that was unsettling.

He continued, "Actually, I like it that way. It feels safe in there, if you know what I mean?"

"'In there'? Actually, I don't know what you mean. Help me understand that, will you?" Dr. Wheatley waited for Ben's response.

"Yeah, in there. When my mom died, it felt like I got hit by a train. I just decided in my heart that I wasn't going to expose myself to any more hurt. So I built a pretty safe little cell to hang out in. This allows me to come out when I need to be with other people, but I can always retreat back into it when I'm done. It works pretty well actually." Ben let out a huge sigh as if he had been holding his breath telling the story. He realized that he had wandered outside of the safety of his cell, and even if it was lonely in there, it was also safe.

"Ben, let me explain something to you that your dad and I have been discussing. I look at grief a little differently than most counselors. For the longest time, we were taught that people experience grief in sequential stages and that, as they pass through those, their grief and pain and life disruption eventually decrease and eventually 'life'"—he added air quotes—"would go back to normal. Whatever normal is!" He paused. "So far, so good, Ben?"

"Yep, I'm with you, and that is all I figured surviving the loss of my mom would be. That I would just need to hang on and hope for the best."

Dr. Wheatley continued, "What we have begun to realize is that grieving is not really as simple as that. It's never simple no matter what anyone does to try to describe a process that is always unique to each person and therefore changing. So, what makes more sense to me, and is supported by plenty of data, is that there are actually 'tasks,' or things we have to do, in each phase of grief, or what I like to call 'season' of grief. I believe that we go through 'seasons' of grief, and just like the physical seasons that we mark time with here in Colorado, each season has specific characteristics attached to it, and each season has certain tools that are more appropriate to use during it as well. The one thing I would have you not miss is the fact that the seasons never really stop. After winter, there's spring, and after spring, there's summer, and after summer, there's fall. But, of course, what comes after fall?" He paused to see if Ben was following him.

Ben was busy trying to take all this in, and he missed the fact that Dr. Wheatley had ended with a question. "Oh wait, you want me to answer that? I mean, it's obvious when you put it that way. Of course, winter comes next. But that's not every hopeful, Doc."

"That's assuming that you do absolutely nothing in each season, right? You describe it as if the seasons will do all the work of healing from the loss you've experienced. I guess it depends on what you will do during each season of your grief. You're currently in the season of winter where everything feels dead and very, very hopeless. That usually leads to us scrambling for ways to contain and control the feelings that we have about the person who is gone. It's such an immense emotional, physical, and psychological hit that our first response is to simply shut down. Everybody does it. In your case, you've ensconced yourself in a cell of your own making in order to contain and control those emotions."

Ben found himself nodding in agreement, realizing that the prison cell picture Dr. Wheatley had painted was resonating with him.

"So, what do I do? I'm not sure that I want to come out and feel all this crap that is swirling inside me. It might hurt someone else, and I can't take that risk!" He could feel the walls of his cell crumbling, but he was furiously working to keep everything in place.

Dr. Wheatley replied, "It's a fair question, Ben. Quite honestly, you don't have to do anything if you don't want to. No one is going to forcibly come into that cell of yours that you find so comfortable yet isolating and make you come out. Does this make sense?"

Ben nodded and cast a glance at his dad again. His dad gave him the thumbs-up sign and went back to listening to Dr. Wheatley.

"On the other hand," Dr. Wheatley continued, "you can choose to come out of your cell at whatever pace you decide you want to. In that case, your dad and I, if you want to continue in counseling, will be here to talk through and explore the seasons of your grief and how you're experiencing them. We were never meant to grieve alone, Ben."

He paused to make sure Ben was following him and saw Ben processing all he was throwing at him. "So what does this all have to do with you? The entire process of mourning is a voluntary one. If it is anything other than that, it won't help very much. So, you get to decide whether to come out of your cell or not. Make sense?" He looked at Ben and waited.

"Yeah, it makes sense, but it's just a lot to take in. I guess I didn't consider the fact that when I exiled myself to my cell, I would be leaving the memories and feelings behind. That's a cost I didn't count on."

At that point, the counseling session came to a pretty quick end. His dad and Wheatley made a next appointment, and they left the office.

—⚬⚭⚬—

We all have reflexive strategies we use to contain and control the immensity of our emotions during the first season of our grief. It can be overwhelming, and it prompts us to rush to do everything we can to keep it all under wraps, just like Ben did. There are a variety of outcomes that appear as a result of these efforts at controlling and containing. One of them is what appears as the disappearance of all emotions. When we shut down like Ben did, our emotions have a main switch that we flip, hoping to keep all the disruptive and powerful emotions at bay.

Take some time today to consider which emotions you have shut down in response to a recent loss you have experienced. Most of our emotions are multilayered. When we're in this season of grief, we will often say, "I don't feel anything." Certainly, at times I'm sure that's the case, but there are other times where we feel the sweetness of the memory we have of the person, and then it turns to sadness, and then it turns to another emotion. That's to be expected. It seems our emotions are often chained together and we are only paying attention to the first link in the chain. If you find it hard to identify your emotions, be patient with yourself and keep an eye out for when you do feel something, then jot down what prompted those feelings.

9

THE AMBIVALENCE
OF GRIEF

*"In these times I don't, in a manner of speaking,
know what I want; perhaps I don't want what I know
and want what I don't know."*
—Marsilio Ficino

"Bob, isn't it wonderful??" Gwen was ecstatic over such a thoughtful gift from Bob's parents in anticipation of their first baby who was due any moment. At least that's how it seemed to Gwen. His parents were incredibly generous people and had told Gwen and Bob to go out and purchase a La-Z-Boy rocker recliner so they would have somewhere comfortable to sit and rock their grandbabies to sleep and read to them.

"Wow! It's amazing. I never thought a chair could be so comfortable!" Bob replied, sitting down in the chair and leaning back. "I think a good nap is calling out to me!" He feigned sleeping and snoring.

"Oh, no you don't!" Gwen playfully punched him in the shoulder. "If anyone needs a nap, it's me. Remember, I'm the one carrying the small human! Enough of this, get out of MY chair!" Gwen was smiling broadly and pulling him by the hand out of the chair.

"Okay, okay, but the minute you give birth and that little human is tyrannizing both of us, it becomes my chair! Got it, young lady?" He had donned a stern face that immediately broke into a laugh.

Bob had lost track of time, and came back to the present realizing that he had been standing looking down at that chair. The memories were hard to shake, and he was immediately pulled back into the past as he stood there transfixed. Slowly he walked over to his desk and sank into his office chair.

Bob sighed a deep sigh and laid his head back into the headrest of the chair. He must have fallen asleep because he was jolted back to reality when he heard, "Dad! Dad!"

It was Ben; he'd come home for the weekend. Bob brightened a bit and smiled at the thought of the young man Ben had become and how fiercely he loved his son. He drew himself out of the chair and walked to the doorway. "Hey, Ben, I'm up here!"

"What are you doing up here?" Ben said as he walked up the stairs. "I thought you might be with your men's group this evening." Ben had gotten home later than he had told his dad he would be home but had expected his dad to still be at his men's group.

"Yeah, I normally would be, but I just wasn't up for social interaction or the awkwardness the guys still seem to feel about what happened with your mom. Either they are awkward, or they end up acting like nothing happened at all. Why is it that guys have such a hard time just being normal around someone who's grieving?" Bob asked, as if he didn't know the answer. Unfortunately, he did because he had been one of those men years before when a friend of his wife had tragically died in a car accident. Looking back on it now, he was embarrassed at his inability to help his friend.

Ben walked into the room and looked around. He was stunned at how much the room looked exactly as his mom had left it. Even her robe was draped over the chair she always sat in to read and have a cup of tea in the evenings.

His dad broke the awkward silence and said, "It's good to have you home, son! Let's go down and get something to eat, shall we? What are you hungry for? Pizza? Specialty sandwiches from Dominos? Or something else?" He smiled weakly as he walked out of the room and headed down the stairway.

"Pizza is fine, Dad. Nothing special. Can I run out and get it?" Ben offered.

"No, no need. You just got home from a long drive from school. Let's just eat in and have pizza and watch a movie. How's that sound to you?" Bob said, reaching for his cell phone on the counter. "Do you mind looking up the number for me?"

"Sure thing." Ben found the number in the app on his phone and read it to his dad.

His dad placed the order, then sighed as if it was a load off not to have to worry about making dinner for the two of them.

The next morning, Ben didn't rush out of bed but instead slept in late. It felt good to not be on a time crunch for a change. Once he dragged himself out of bed and down to the kitchen, he poured himself a cup of coffee and walked out on the deck where it looked like his dad was deep in thought. As he sat down, he noticed that tears were running down his dad's cheeks. He took a couple of sips of his coffee and just settled into the chair looking out across the lawn.

As Bob wiped away the tear that had found its way down his check, he said, "Good morning, Ben. How'd you sleep?"

"Oh fine, Dad. It felt good to sleep in and not have to get up to go to a class," Ben answered, wondering if he should broach the topic of his dad's tears or not.

"So, what's up, Dad? What's going on?" He looked over at his dad to check to see if there were any more tears.

"Oh, I don't know. Actually I do know. It's that stupid chair in our bedroom. The base has broken, and I don't see a way to repair it. That's what I was up in our room trying to figure out when you came home last night. It seems like such a minor thing. It's just a chair, I keep telling myself, but I feel like I'm back at the night we came home from the hospital without your mom. There are just so many memories that are bombarding me all at once. It feels like someone has ripped the bandages off my heart, and it just hurts all over again. I have made no progress at all in this recovery. Actually, in many ways, I'm not entirely convinced that I want to 'recover.'" He added air quotes just to make a sarcastic point about the word. "It seems to me that it's one thing to have your mom die and be gone, but to recover or heal, or whatever word you want to use, just means losing her all over again. It's a double loss, and I just don't want to go through it. If you didn't notice, I've done absolutely nothing to change our room nor taken her clothes out of the closet. If you had looked in the bathroom, you would have found that everything has been left just as she left it before she went to the hospital for the last time." He paused and looked down at his journal and quickly closed it.

When we are approached by people in our lives who communicate to us the importance of grieving our losses and moving on, their words of advice or even encouragement are fraught with danger more so than they know. Ben's dad points out a very important feature of allowing our grief to take its course. When you are grieving, you will find that there is the initial shock of losing a loved one, but then there is the rest of the journey to undertake. Before long, though, we realize that this process leads us to a final good-bye, and that is what we often find ourselves fighting. Therefore, there is an intense ambivalence about walking the journey of grief. We realize that in order to heal we need to take this journey, but we also know that taking this journey threatens our sense of the other person in our life.

It is not uncommon to get stuck early on in the journey of grief since at some level the pain of loss reminds us of the importance of the person in our lives. Give yourself permission to rest from your pain, and then at other times, push into it because ultimately the love and grace of God is waiting for you to help you grow from the loss you have endured. It's too early for that just now, but be patient. Embrace the journey. Learn from those around you.

10

AVOIDANCE OR PURSUIT?

"You get hit the hardest when trying to run or hide from a problem. Like the defense on a football field, putting all focus on evading only one defender is asking to be blindsided."
—Criss Jami

The summer passed by faster than Ben had expected. He had gotten an unpaid internship with a social media company and learned a lot about the inner workings of a company like that. He and his dad held steady in just busying themselves with the work at hand, and didn't talk much about the counseling session, although Ben could never stop thinking about the prison cell he had built for himself. The more he thought about it, the more he realized how it described his experience in trying to manage the percolating emotions that were underneath his facade of being good-natured, laid-back, and hardworking.

When August hit, Ben began the preparation for going back to school for one more year—his senior year. What a big deal! In spite of the fact that he was a business major, he was enrolled in a psychology class that he had heard about from other students. He had heard so many of them rave about this class on grief and loss, but at this point in his life he was unconvinced that he was not even remotely interested in going to a class like that. He had made a commitment to himself that he would go to the first few classes, and then he would figure out if there was anything else he could substitute for the class that at least sounded more enjoyable than those subjects. It wasn't as if he hadn't had enough of them for a lifetime! The class sounded downright depressing, and he wondered why so many students found it so interesting.

The first day of class came, and he looked around for anyone he knew in the class, then settled into a seat next to a friend of his who was a psych major and was his roommate during freshman year. Since that first year, they had gone different directions with friend groups more within their own majors, so Ben had lost track of what had been happening in Tony's life.

"Ben! What are you doing in a class like this? This would be the last place I would expect to find you!" Tony was smiling broadly and got up to give him a hug.

"Hey man, how ya doing?" Ben was caught off guard by the hug. It was unsettling because it felt like someone had invaded his prison cell, and he found himself hating it and appreciating it at the same time.

"I'm doing okay. As for the class, you among others recommended it to me, and I had an elective to fill, so here I am. I figured that I would see how it goes for the first few classes and then decide if I'm staying or not," Ben replied.

"Got it. That's fair. Like I told you when I had heard from 'reliable sources'"—he made air quotes with his fingers—"about this class, I've been so pumped to have the opportunity to take it finally. I think you'll find the prof to be unlike any you've heard in the school of business. By the way, how's your mom doing? The last time I saw you, she was in remission from the breast cancer."

Tony was busy checking something on his phone, so he didn't look up, but Ben was thankful because he wasn't quite ready to engage the conversation in depth with anyone at this point. "Thanks for checking, Tony, but last spring she passed away. The cancer was pretty aggressive when it came back, and it wasn't long before she died." Ben bit his lip because suddenly the emotions were storming his cell door.

"Oh man, Ben. I'm so sorry to hear that. I'd love to hear more about it when we have more time. Would you be up for that later?" Tony's face had completely changed to utter concern and compassion for what Ben had just told him. Ben had to bite his lip again.

"Okay folks, let's get going!" The prof was starting the class, so Ben just nodded and they turned their attention to what the prof had to say about the requirements for the class, the way the class was going to be conducted, and the variety of assignments that students would be expected to complete by semester's end.

A couple of days later, Tony and Ben found some time to sit on the patio of one of the academic buildings on campus. They got a cup of coffee and headed for one of the empty tables in the shade of the building.

"So whaddya think after hearing what the class is going to be like, Ben?" Tony jumped in without missing a beat from their conversation just before class.

"It was fine. I mean it wasn't bad at all. The assignment load doesn't seem that tough compared to some of the business classes I've had. But I'm not sure I'm ready to head into this subject area just yet. What do you think?" Ben asked.

"Boy, do I get that in terms of the subject area! Don't fall asleep on the journals each week, though. Just remember, with this particular prof it's not about academic output as much as it is about what he calls the landscape of your heart. I know that kind of sounds watered down, but the further in you go, you realize how little time you actually spend in your heart. It seems like school is all about gaining more information on some subject rather than our heart development. With this prof, it's completely upside down, and that's a little hard to get used to coming from another major." Tony looked across the table to see if Ben was tracking with him.

The conversation moved on from comparing notes about classes, the latest sports scores and the other classes that they each had. It was getting near to dinner time, so they each had a commitment to go to prior to dinner, so they parted company.

When Ben got home, he sat down and took a deep breath. At that moment, he just wished he could hear his mom's voice one more time. He wanted to talk to her and tell her how school was starting up.

He reached for the notebook he had impulsively bought on the way home from his meeting with Tony. He opened it to the first page and wrote, "Dear Mom, I really miss you." He couldn't get much further before the tears flowed and he couldn't see the paper any longer.

While many perspectives on grief always start with talking about denial, we often don't get the full explanation of what the word denial actually means. It means so much more than a this-can't-be-happening kind of refusal to acknowledge what's happening. We often find ourselves wrestling with not only the fact of things feeling surreal but also the meaning of losing the person we love so much. It means so much more than just the fact that he or she is gone. Often, it's this meaning that tempts us into what Ben did, and that's run away. Interestingly enough, when we're being chased by a mountain lion, like here in the Rocky Mountains where I live, any direction away from the predator will do to accomplish our safety. That is often the same approach we take with our grief. The other side of that coin is, if we continue the metaphor of being chased by a wild animal, if we knew of a cabin a safe distance away that would provide protection for us, then we would no doubt pursue the path that would take us to that cabin. It's not just any direction that will do. It's a specific direction that will take us to safety, and we will take a straight path to achieve it.

The same thing is true for grief recovery and the role of denial in it. Denial is taking whatever path will take you away from the pain of the grief you feel. Whatever it takes to reduce the pain is all that matters. On the other hand, if you want to pursue healing of your grief, then there is a particular path you need to take, and that path involves leaning into the pain rather than fleeing from it.

11

FEELINGS? WHAT FEELINGS?

*"There can be no transforming of darkness into light and
of apathy into movement without emotion."*
—Carl Gustav Jung

When she woke up, Joy knew something was dramatically wrong. At least she assumed that it was. In the months leading up to today, her usual routine was to wake up, roll her eyes (because it was another day like the last one), sigh at the challenge of the day, and then stumble downstairs and pour herself a cup of coffee. Often she would sit in the sun on the back deck and summon her emotional and physical resources for what the day was going to throw at her. The one thing that was consistently absent was overwhelming emotions. Granted, there were times where she would get hijacked by them in one-off situations, like the stroller going past the house, but generally she felt numb. More often than not, the numbness was a welcome friend.

Today was different. It felt like her emotions were on fire. Somehow they had awakened and went from numb to very much alive. She lay in bed hoping it would pass like other times in the past; it felt like everything hurt. It wasn't a physical hurt of any kind. No matter where her thoughts took her, the profound pain of Aaron's absence seemed to be meeting her head-on. What was happening?

As she rolled out of bed, poured herself a cup of coffee, and headed out to the deck, she thought about her journey so far. Her friend Meg had explained to her that she was in what she called the "winter of grief," when everything is cold and numb and the grieving person cycles through different types of denial. This includes denial of the importance of the person, which really wasn't Joy's problem. Probably the biggest thing she wrestled with was accepting the reality she was actually living in, rather than going off on a variety of tangents that her friends had either modeled or tempted her with. Up to this point, she thought she had been doing a reasonably good job of accepting her reality as it was not as she would want it, which meant having Aaron back in her life. But now, with her feelings seemingly coming online, she began to wonder if her evaluation of her acceptance was all that accurate.

She went in search of her phone, which she had left in the kitchen, and found Meg's phone number in her Favorites folder in her phone.

She dialed the number and waited. "Hi, Meg! It's Joy. Hey, I was wondering if you would have some time in the next couple of days to get another walk in to talk about something?"

"Well, hi, Joy! What a pleasant surprise to hear from you. Sure, I've got a window of time tomorrow afternoon to take a walk. You want me to just walk by your house, and we can pick up from there?" Meg responded.

"Sounds good to me, Meg! Thanks so much. I look forward to it! See you then." Joy hit the end button on her phone.

Joy returned to her book on the deck, but after looking at it a moment, she decided she'd rather just take a walk by herself.

She chartered a different course than she had taken with Meg, just to change things up a bit. The problem was that it ended up being longer than she expected.

"Hey, Mom and Dad! I'm home!" Joy yelled into the kitchen as she came in the front door.

"We're back here just getting dinner on!" her mom yelled back.

Joy hung up her backpack and ran upstairs to retrieve her tablet to do some reading later. As she came back down the stairs, she wondered how her parents were doing. She had been focused on her own recovery and had given little thought to how they might have been affected by their grandchild's death. Joy made a mental note to check in with both of them soon. She had been spending more time with her mom than her dad because of his work, but she sensed that something was up. He had been strong and helping everyone but giving very little away about how losing a grandson was affecting him.

The next afternoon, Joy wasn't working at the library, so as before, she loaded up her travel mug with coffee and waited on the porch for Meg to round the bend into their neighborhood. As she approached, Joy walked down the steps to meet her on the sidewalk.

"Good afternoon, Joy!" Meg greeted her. "A beautiful day, isn't it?"

"Yep, served right up for our walk-and-talk sessions!" Joy smiled broadly. It was good to see Meg again. There was a certain comfort in their conversations that made Joy feel free to say whatever was on her heart, even if it was tough stuff, she knew Meg wasn't going to back away.

"So, what's up, Joy, other than your insatiable need to be around my sparkling personality?" Meg chuckled.

"Oh stop, Meg! If there's any bright spot or gift from God I have during this season of grief, as you so often refer to it, you're it. I'm so thankful for your willingness to walk—literally and figuratively—through it with me," Joy replied.

She continued, "I woke up yesterday morning feeling like all my emotions had cranked up to levels I had never felt before. I was assuming that I was doing everything right in terms of my grief, and this completely took me off guard. Any thoughts? " Joy asked.

"Yeah, actually I do . . . I'm sure that's a surprise, right?" Meg answered and smiled again. "In all seriousness, while I'm sure this may not come as any consolation, you are actually moving into another season of grief. Remember when I talked to you way back when we first met, that one way to think about grief is in terms of seasons, right?"

"Yes, actually that stuck with me, Meg. You said then that I was in the winter of my grief, when everything is numb and cold and dark. I have come to see just how vividly true that was," Joy said.

"Yep, exactly! I'm glad it was helpful. But imagine if we stayed in winter all year round. It would be a pretty depressing place, wouldn't it?" Meg glanced over at Joy to see her nodding.

"The usefulness of thinking of our grief in terms of seasons is that we often look forward to the next one, right? After a while, winter gets pretty heavy and weary, and we begin to look forward to spring. Well, it appears that that's what you are heading into, the spring of your grief. The thing is that with seasons in the physical world, they often intermingle. We will have a springlike day in winter and a very winter-like day in spring. If you think about it, spring is kind of a transitional season between winter and summer, so it has features of both. The key to keep in mind is that in the spring of our grief, our emotions seem to wake up, just like the trees and flowers bloom. Admittedly, it's a mixed bag since we aren't so sure that we want those emotions to wake up because, as you said, they bring pain—and happiness—with them."

Joy had a lot to think about after her walk. She had never heard the idea of emotions "waking up," but it certainly explained a lot of her current experiences. Somehow it felt a little different to know that this was to be expected rather than getting hijacked by these emotions she was having. Her talks with Meg had helped to put some things about her grief into perspective, and that had helped her to set her expectations a little more realistically.

The spring of our grief is an important time in our journey through grief. We have been hanging on and often just focusing on surviving winter, but when spring appears, it brings with it the emotions that have not had much expression during winter. It's an important time to begin to explore those feelings and continue the healing journey of grief.

12

PLATITUDES

"Usually when you are grieving and someone says something so senselessly optimistic to you, it's about them. Either they want to feel like they can say something helpful, or they simply cannot allow themselves to entertain the finality and pain of death, so instead they turn it into a Precious Moments greeting card."
—Nadia Bolz-Weber

Joy had taken a huge risk by going out with a few friends from her time in college. It was a risk because they were not terribly reliable when it came to empathy. As is often the case for people who have nothing to say, they substitute nothing for some kind of statement of comparison trying to make the situation sound better than it is.

At the same time, she had been encouraged to try to get back into life again, but she was uncertain if this was such a good idea.

Joy had a group of friends she had met at the university she went to, and they had hung out all the time until she found out she was pregnant, and then they all melted away. They never directly "ghosted" her, but every time she tried to check in with them, they would always have something else to do when she tried to set something up.

Finally, her friend Lauren reached out to her and invited her to get together with the group saying, "Just like old times!"

Joy took a deep breath as she pulled up to the brewery they would often frequent in their college days. She was living at home now, but it was relatively close to the town her university was in, so it was an easy drive to get there. Joy checked in with the staff and made her way to the booth where her friends were all sitting. Lauren, the first to see her coming, jumped out of the booth and ran to meet her.

"Joy! It's so good to see you again! I'm glad you could come."

Joy was a little amazed that Lauren was acting as if nothing had happened and they were picking up where they had left off a few years ago.

"Hi, Lauren! Thanks so much for inviting me! It's helpful to get out after losing Aaron. I could use a change of pace."

Joy noted a brief expression change in Lauren that signaled she wasn't expecting to hear her refer to her little boy. "Oh, let's not talk about that right now. There's time for that later. Now's the time to enjoy getting to know you again. It's been so long!"

"Yes, of course. Thanks again for inviting me." They were walking back to the booth, and the other friends all got out and gave Joy a huge hug. It was comforting to Joy, but she was on her guard for what was coming next.

During dinner, they each took turns sharing all the changes that had happened over the last few years. Joy had been pretty quiet during the whole thing even though she was enjoying hearing what was going on in their lives.

Joy took a deep breath and thought, It's time to own what's happened and allow others to hear about it. I know from my conversations with Meg that when I speak it, I own it as a reality that I need to accept.

"Well, it has been an eventful few years, to be sure. You guys remember that I was hanging out with Caleb, I mean, I was pretty consumed with Caleb. He was so wonderful and kind, but after a while he started pushing my boundaries in every way possible, including physically. He kept pushing, and eventually I gave in and we had sex."

Joy was watching them, and it appeared that they were tracking with her.

Robin was the first to speak, "Wow, Joy, that must have been really tough trying to hold off that kind of pressure. I've faced that, too, and I did the same thing. It's something I am not at all proud of, but it's really tough when you think you are going to lose a good relationship."

Joy nodded and thought, *Maybe this is going to be better than I thought.*

She continued, "Well, I thought that would get him off my back, but it only got worse. I felt an immense amount of shame over it all and didn't dare talk to anyone else about it. Unfortunately, a few weeks later my period didn't start, and I got suspicious. I waited just to be sure, and about a week later I took a pregnancy test, and sure enough, I was pregnant."

Her friends looked shocked. They said nothing, so she kept charging on.

"The pregnancy went pretty well, including all the usual morning sickness, but overall it was good. Then when I was due, something started happening. Actually, it was something stopped happening. My little boy stopped moving, and they rushed me into a C-section only to find out that he had his umbilical cord wrapped around his little neck, and he had died.

"It's been about five months now since he died, and I'm still trying to recover from the hole in my heart that was left behind." Her eyes filled with tears, and she wiped them away. "I'm so sorry to bring down the mood today, but it's my story and is in many ways all-consuming, as you can imagine."

Jill spoke up. "Joy, I'm so sorry you had to go through that, but I've always heard it said that time heals all wounds. Maybe you need to just wait it out, and it'll get better."

Joy nodded but felt like someone had just slapped her and suggested that her tears and sadness were going to "get better."

Becca nodded in agreement with Jill and then added, "Well, at least you were able to get pregnant, I've known a lot of people who struggle with getting pregnant. It took my cousin three years to finally get pregnant, and it was devastating to her."

Robin jumped into the conversation. "When I've gone through some pretty tough times myself, which you all know about, and I had someone at church speak Romans 8:28 over me, which reminds us that in all things God works for good. I needed to be reminded of that."

She looked expectantly at Joy as if to suggest that what she was saying was profound enough to make the sadness and situation better.

Joy was stunned. She wiped her tears away and changed the subject to the future plans of each of her friends. It was pretty clear that they didn't want to talk any more about what had happened to her.

Platitudes are often seen as "ghost sentences." In other words, there is what is actually said, and then there is what is actually meant. These phrases seem to reduce a catastrophic and unfixable problem to something that can be fixed. The most important part to keep in mind during interactions like this is that most often platitudes are about the other person's pain and confusion rather than a genuine desire to respond to yours. It's a little bit like trying to cover a bullet wound with a Band-Aid.

Unfortunately, platitudes are most often present during this spring season of your grief and have the greatest impact because you are starting to feel again, and it seems that you are even more vulnerable than before to comments like the ones Joy got from her friends. Be careful to attach the problem not to yourself but rather to the others' inability to empathize with you even though they may be convinced that Scripture *should* make a difference in your feelings and conclusions. Just remember that an ill-timed truth (a platitude) is experienced by the other person as a weapon. If you're at all like Joy, you can easily get hijacked by well-meaning friends, so don't blame yourself for others' insensitivity. You are not a problem to be fixed, but a person to care for!

13

THE TYRANNY OF
"IF ONLY"

*"There were so many places in my time with (him) that
I wished I could go back to, hitting the stop button at just one
moment to stop everything that came after. I had so many
If Onlys, but each place I thought to stop meant missing
something that came later. I needed it all, in the end,
to make my own story find its finish."*
—Sarah Dessen

Joy felt something odd in her belly as she was getting up one morning. She didn't think anything of it and just chalked it up to being pregnant for the first time. So she went through the remainder of her day, and as she sat reading a book about the first months with a baby, she felt that strange feeling again, but it wasn't because something was happening, it was because something wasn't happening. Her baby was strangely quiet, and it concerned her. She called her obstetrician and described what was going on, and her doctor said to come to the ER immediately.

It was at that point that Joy woke up with a jerk. She immediately started crying. The kind of crying where you can't catch your breath or get a word out to anyone. All she could do was cry, as that seemed to be the only adequate expression of the depth of pain she was experiencing *again*. The longer she thought about it, her sorrow and pain turned into a deep self-loathing for what she should have done. The thoughts virtually cascaded like a waterfall tumbling down a rock face. *What if I had gone to the hospital sooner? What if I had paid attention to the warning signs? What if I had been more careful with sleep and stress? What if I had been more careful with the drinks I had during the pregnancy? I only had two the entire nine months, but still. Did I eat something that caused it? C'mon, God, what did I do to make this happen?* They kept coming like a relentless firehose of shame and self-blame.

She heard a gentle knock on her door, and her mom's voice on the other side of the door. "Joy, honey, is everything okay? I heard you crying."

"C'mon in, Mom," Joy said with immense resignation that this whole grieving thing was never going to end. She had been sure that by this time she wouldn't be having these dreams. It was six months, almost seven, since Aaron's death; weren't these dreams ever going to stop?

Joy's mom came in and sat on the bed near her. "Was it one of those replay dreams again? The one where you stopped it from happening?"

"Yep, pretty much," Joy replied in the middle of her tears continuing to tumble down her face. Her weeping had morphed into just a steady stream of tears.

"I'm guessing you're thinking that these dreams and painful memories should be over by now?" her mom asked.

"Yeah, how long is this going to take, Mom? This is getting downright ridiculous. I mean, I'm going on seven months since Aaron died. Why does this have to be so hard?"

Her mom nodded. "Yeah, I couldn't agree more, sweetheart. Our minds and hearts just can't wrap around the immensity of what has happened. There's an awful hole that has been left behind that Aaron once inhabited. We want with all our hearts to fill that hole with a redo of history, with explanations, and even distractions. That's probably why these dreams are coming up for you. You're trying to fill a hole that has been left behind with some kind of action that would have prevented it. It's a natural part of grieving for us as humans. So, I guess the answer to your question, 'Why does this have to be so hard?' is because you loved your little boy so fiercely."

"As much as I 'understand' what you are saying, I am finding myself creating all kinds of expectations according to what I want in the moment rather than actually validating the love I had for him, and the pain, dreams, and emotions are only an indication of that rather than an indication that something is dreadfully wrong." Joy looked up from her feet that she had been studying to her mom.

"I would agree, there is a difference between 'knowing' and understanding the grief we experience. I certainly understand what you mean, and your dad and I struggle with it too. If only we had been more watchful with you, then maybe Aaron would be here in your arms. The 'if onlys' are meant to turn back time so that we can do it over and get it right. Unfortunately, that doesn't change the reality we are living in. They can be pretty nasty in how they taunt us away from the reality we are trying to cope with."

"No, no, Mom," Joy replied quickly. "There was nothing you or dad could have done. You guys have been nothing but supportive, and for that I'm eternally grateful."

During the springtime of our grief the emotions wake up just like during this season in nature when plants, and even animals that have been in hibernation, awake and become more active. With these emotions comes a variety of strategies we tend to use to minimize their impact on us. We might have thought during the winter season of our grief that we were going to be able to get out of this grieving thing unscathed, but it is often our emotions that will not be denied. One of the strategies is to alter history in order to achieve the outcome we so desperately desired. This, too, is to be expected in our journey through grief. It is not something to criticize or condemn ourselves for.

Another aspect of this that Joy illustrates is our tendency to believe that knowing is understanding. Interestingly, in Matthew 13:18 Jesus has just finished telling a series of parables that leaves the disciples scratching their heads. One of the most popular parables Jesus taught was the parable of the sower. As Jesus explains it to the disciples, he actually describes a group of people who hear but don't "understand." The actual Greek word for "understand" means to "put together." In other words, taking the time to take what we "know," or hear, and fit it together with other bits of wisdom and guidance we have received over time. Understanding our grief isn't about knowing the stages, or the seasons, of grief. Knowing only takes us so far. It's taking that knowledge and pushing it into our experience in such a way that we truly understand it.

One of the biggest challenges for people walking the journey of grief and its seasons is moving beyond what they know about grief to actually living it out. That is where understanding and wisdom are waiting for us.

So, be patient with your growing "understanding" of your own journey of grief. Unfortunately, it takes time and a commitment to learn about the landscape of our own grief and the seasons we are experiencing.

14

TEARS

Days after Joy had her fateful meeting with her college friends, she was consumed with reviewing what had happened with her pregnancy. So, when Meg called to go for a walk with her, Joy eagerly accepted.

As was her habit, Joy was waiting on the front porch as Meg was coming down her street.

"Hey, Joy! Good to see you. I've been wondering how you've been doing for a while, and I finally got around to talking you into walking and talking. Funny how those two go together," Meg said as she approached Joy's house.

"Yeah, yeah, don't try to guilt me into doing this more often!" Joy smiled. She appreciated the emotional safety her relationship with Meg offered her.

"No guilt from me! That's all on you. I would never think of getting you to do anything through guilt. I'd just ask you." Meg winked at her with a smirk.

"Well, I actually had something happen a few weeks ago that I'm still running over in my mind, trying to figure out what went wrong." Joy launched into telling Meg about her lunch with her college friends.

"I remembered what you and others have said, that it's a good idea to launch out a little to re-establish old friendships that have been lost or engage some new ones that could provide the network to support me while I go through my grief."

"Yep, that's pretty much correct," Meg said, "but it's important to make sure that the people you are talking to have some measure of understanding of what you are attempting to do. Otherwise, most people will just plaster you with platitudes that only make matters worse."

"Well, that's exactly what happened," Joy replied. "It was unspeakably painful to hear such trite phrases—sorry if I sound mean—that seem to be just slapping over such a devastating event. It cheapened it, and on top of it all, I started to cry."

They had turned the corner, and Joy could hardly see for the tears that were welling up in her eyes. She slowed her pace to try to compose herself.

"Let's unpack this, shall we?" Meg began. "First, platitudes are a substitute for wisdom and also serve the purpose of helping the person dispensing it feel like she is doing something helpful. Second, let's get something really clear about tears and grief, shall we? Culturally, we see tears as an indication of our weakness, our insensitivity to others, and the indicator that we are 'falling apart.' Meg emphasized this with air quotes. Between you and me, this is probably one of the things that makes me the most frustrated about the people who are well-intentioned in trying to help us, and they, too, see tears as something being profoundly wrong. Are you following me so far?"

"Absolutely," Joy responded, thankful for the emotional break from reporting about her meeting with her friends.

"Good, so let me get one thing really clear, but to do that let me ask you a question." Meg looked expectantly at Joy.

"Go for it. I think I'm recovered from my recent melt-down." Joy smiled weakly.

"Meltdown? What meltdown? You mean when you shed the tears over the pain you felt? This is an example of what I was talking about when I said we see tears as an indication of our weakness or falling apart. But I'll let it pass for now." Meg winked at her.

She continued, "How much did you love Aaron?"

Joy gasped at the sound of his name, but there was a certain comfort in knowing that someone else remembered him too. "What do you mean, Meg? That's a really strange question to me!" She was confused, and she was afraid of another plati-tude but didn't believe that Meg would do such a thing.

"Listen, Joy, I want you to see something, but I can't without establishing some key concepts. So just humor me. I promise it will lead somewhere important. Trust me." Meg had slowed her pace as well and was looking at Joy steadily as she motioned for them to stop at a nearby bench to sit.

Joy answered her question. "I can't measure the amount of my love for Aaron. That would simply be impossible. Those nine months I had with him, even though he was in my belly, were my first indication of what my relationship with him would be once he was born. I knew that he knew my voice, and I couldn't wait to hear his. Then there's all the dreams I had about what life would be like with him, about him growing up, toddlerhood, elementary school, and all the rest. My love is connected to all that."

"So, what if I told you that the tears you shed are directly proportional to the entire fabric of your relationship with Aaron?" Meg paused to make sure Joy was with her.

"Okay?" Joy's voice trailed off, her mind walking back into history and all the dreams and memories she'd had.

"Here's another question, Joy. How have you felt in the past when someone you'd only met in one of your classes died?"

"Now, since I've experienced loss, or before?" Joy asked.

"Let's say before you ever had Aaron. I know that is hard because your life has so dramatically changed since then, but give it a shot."

Joy paused. "I do remember hearing about a student I had shared a business class with who died in an accident. I was sad for his family, but only in a distant, socially approved sort of way. To say that I felt any specific feelings about it would be lying."

"Okay, so let's go one step further. Did you shed any tears for that student you heard had died?" Meg was posing a comparison between the two people, her son and this acquaintance, which for Joy wasn't even realistic.

"Of course not! I wasn't close to him at all, I just shared a classroom with him. That was it." Joy was beginning to get irritated with this line of questioning. She wished Meg would just tell her what she was getting at.

"Okay, so you have shed many tears over Aaron because you loved him and were close to him, but for the other student you didn't have any tears, right?" Meg seemed to be getting closer, so Joy was going to be patient.

"Yes, exactly. Where is this going, Meg? The suspense is killing me!"

Meg nodded, realizing that she was drawing this out longer than Joy had the patience for. "It's simply this. Tears are connected to those we love, and when we prohibit such expression, we are prohibiting the grieving person from expressing their love for the person they have lost. It simply doesn't make sense. I have come to realize that when I apologize for my tears over losing my husband, I am apologizing for the intense love I had for him. It simply doesn't make sense. When I first realized that, it all became clear and I found freedom in allowing my tears to flow. I have come to the decision that I will never apologize for my tears again. It would be like apologizing for my relationship with Henry, and I refuse to do that."

It was like a bomb went off in Joy's heart, filled with a new level of fierce love and loyalty to Aaron and her love for him. She, too, would learn from this and refuse to apologize for her tears even if it made everyone else around her uncomfortable.

One of the ways that we manage the newly experienced pain of our grief is through "stuffing" our tears, or if we can't do that, we tend to apologize for them. But we have to ask, why do we do that? Why do we apologize or hide our tears? Somehow the hurting person starts taking care of the comforter rather than the other way around. Some of the reason is related to how we see our own pain and grief. We see it as something abnormal that other people *shouldn't* have to deal with. It is far easier to take care of someone else than to validate our own pain from loss. The important thing to keep in mind is that your emotions are not something you have to spare others from experiencing. There *are* some people out there who are more comfortable with your tears than you are and who are willing to create a space for you to safely experience your loss. Unfortunately, the only way to find them is to move toward changing your own view of your grief, remind yourself that the emotions you are now experiencing are thoroughly human, and embrace the freedom that is yours to express them in the presence of emotionally safe people.

15

OKAY . . . NOW I'M ANGRY!

"Everything that irritates us about others can lead us to an understanding of ourselves."

—Carl Jung

"Whoa, whoa, whoa! Back up the bus . . . what is going on with you?" Joy's dad was reacting to her outburst. He was looking at her with concern. Just minutes before, he had made an observation about someone in his office who had an interaction with him about a project they were working on together. He said something about how the other person's heart just didn't seem fully in the project, and they were both getting busted by their supervisor about shoddy work. As Joy listened, she started to feel more and more frustrated with her dad's insensitivity and harshness about his coworker.

All of a sudden, she couldn't hold it in any longer, "Dad! Why do you have to be so mean to that person? You have no idea what might be going on with her! You're being really unfair and cruel!"

You would have thought that her dad had gotten hit by a two-by-four. He looked stunned, hurt, and surprised all in the same expression. He closed the lid of his computer and looked up at her.

"Joy, what's going on? You've been pretty irritable the last week or so. I don't understand. It seems like no matter what I say, it gets under your skin. Can you help me out here?" He looked at her expectantly. It wasn't anger coming back at her from him; he looked genuinely confused.

"I guess you're right, Dad. I was walking with Meg the other day, and we were talking about how all of a sudden it seems like all my emotions are in overdrive and amplified to such a degree that it seems like the littlest things can make me irritated and just downright angry."

Joy reflected on the last week since she had seen Meg. It seemed that the trend of intensity had risen ever since she had talked to her. While she thought she understood what Meg was talking about in terms of the reawakening of her emotions, she really didn't like it leaking out on the people she loved. "I'm sorry, Dad. I guess I'm just living on a razor's edge with my feelings, and it seems like the smallest things will trigger a reaction that is really out of proportion with the situation."

Her dad nodded his head in understanding. "You know, Joy, I was just reading a book the other day that was talking about grieving the loss of someone you love. I know that I didn't have the relationship with your baby like you did, but I'll admit I had begun to build images, hopes, and dreams for what the future would be like with Aaron." He paused as he began to be overcome with his own emotions.

He looked down to compose his thoughts and feelings. Tears began to fill his eyes. He looked up at Joy choking back the tears as he spoke. "I had entertained so many scenarios of holding him, and putting him to sleep, and eventually taking him on walks . . ." His voice trailed off in a rush of dreams that would never be. He was quiet for a long time as the tears rolled down his cheeks.

"I'm so sorry that you have to go through this, but please remember that you don't have to go through it alone. I can certainly say that I have had my own share of anger over the way things have turned out. I have spent more drives home ranting at God for putting my daughter through what you have been through and leaving this gaping hole in all our hearts, but most of all yours." He paused again to regain his composure.

"Listen, in no way am I mad at what you said or the anger you feel with God and everyone else, for that matter. I certainly understand it. I sure don't feel like you do, but I do feel the pain of his absence."

"So, let me complete my thought about what I was reading. The author said that it was actually very normal and expected for us to feel anger mixed with our grief. You mentioned to me that Meg has been talking to you about the seasons of your grief, and I think this author said something very similar. He said that as our feelings awake, one of the first to show up and make it presence known is anger." He looked up at Joy to see how she was doing.

Joy was quietly weeping with her dad and haltingly said, "Thanks, Dad, for sharing that. I was wondering how you were doing with all this. You just seem to spend most of your time taking care of everyone else, but I'll admit it didn't seem like it was affecting you very much. I now see that you're really good at shouldering the emotional weight that we have all been feeling. I guess I would love to hear more sometime soon."

"I'd welcome that, Joy. I think you know that I'm not going to be put off by your anger. It's your feelings, and I'll let them be your feelings rather than mine. One of the things I'm beginning to learn in real time is that losing someone you love prompts a natural reaction to place blame somewhere, and that's what I think each of us is feeling in our own way. That's what the anger does for us. It's better to speak it than to have it poison us and our relationships. I heard someone once say, 'Holding on to anger is like grasping a hot coal with the intent of throwing it at someone else; you are the one who gets burned.' It makes sense, doesn't it?"

Joy nodded and walked over to her dad, who got up as she approached. They embraced a long time with more tears being shed that they both needed to release.

The spring of our grief brings emotions to the surface that have been "frozen" in place during the winter. They seem to come out of hibernation with a ravenous hunger to be expressed. Anger is the one that frightens us the most because of how potentially alienating it can be. Will it leak out into relationships with people we care the most about? Yes, of course it will. Trying to stuff it will only lead to an insidious poisoning of our emotional systems. Yet, at the same time, it is important to find key safe people in your world who have good enough boundaries not to take offense at your anger or personalize your anger as if it is all about them. It isn't. It's about the condition of your broken heart. The safe people in your world will give you permission to have your anger and stay with you in it. Ultimately, that will give you permission to accept (again) your own helplessness and anger over what has happened. As you slowly begin to embrace that helplessness, you will find that the journey will continue, but it won't feel quite so isolating.

16

MEMORIAL OR MEMORIES?

"Death leaves a heartache no one can heal.
Love leaves a memory no one can steal."
—Irish Headstone

The text sound on Ben's phone went off as he was leaving class. It read, "Hey, Ben! I'm in town for a week, you want to get together?"

The text was from a high school friend of Ben's named Craig Scott. They had played football together for the two years that Ben had played football, which were his junior and senior years of high school. Craig completely fit the stereotype of a football jock. He hung out with a completely different group of kids than Ben, but they had forged a relationship around football, and both seemed to straddle each other's respective peer groups. After high school, Craig went to another state school on a football scholarship and had done pretty well for himself. He was playing on the football team for his school and was their starting safety on defense.

Ben was a little surprised to hear from Craig since he thought when they had drifted apart that there was little chance he would hear from him ever again.

Ben replied, "Sure, when are you available?"

"How about Friday, late afternoon?" was the reply.

"Where do you want to meet?" Ben texted.

"How about we meet at that little coffee shop by your campus? I don't mind driving."

"Sounds good, see you then!" Ben wondered what this was all about, but he had another class to get to, so he didn't give it much thought until Friday afternoon rolled around and he was walking to the coffee shop.

When he got there, he walked in and looked around trying to spot Craig.

"Hey, Ben! Over here." Craig waved from a corner table.

Ben walked over and shook his hand, and they embraced. Craig, being the massive human that he was gave him a bear hug that almost emptied the air from his lungs. Ben stepped back and moved to the other side of the table from Craig.

"I'll tell you what, give me a minute and I'm going to order something," Ben said pointing at the counter.

After completing his order, he walked back to where Craig was sitting. He knew his name was going to be called at any minute, so he sat on the edge of his seat ready to run to the bar to get his iced latte. After that ritual was complete, he returned to the table and settled in to the table with Craig.

"So, Ben, how's it going? I heard about your mom from social media and thought it would be a good time to connect again."

"It's going okay, I guess. Oh, thanks for reaching out, Craig. It was a pleasant but unexpected surprise, to be sure."

Craig nodded in agreement. "Yeah, I certainly get that. I don't know if you heard, but my grandfather passed away about a year ago. I was really close to him, and it really knocked me back. I had a pretty hard time coming back from it. As a matter of fact, I was so angry at everyone and everything that I pretty much isolated myself. The only thing I did which allowed me to distract from my emotions was football."

"I guess I didn't know that, Craig. I'm so sorry. I think I remember you talking about your grandpa. At the time, he seemed larger than life itself, and you really looked up to him." As soon as the words were out of his mouth, Ben immediately saw the parallel between his situation and Craig's.

"Yep, that's pretty much a good description of my grandpa. He had had so many experiences that made him seem all-powerful, and all-knowing too, even though he could be cantankerous at times." Craig's emotions seemed nearer than when they started their conversation, and Ben caught the look on Craig's face as one of a mixture of pain but also pleasant memories.

"Even though it's been over a year ago, the pain comes rushing back in waves now and again, but that's okay. The pain is connected to the love I had for him, and denying it would be denying how much I loved him."

Ben nodded in agreement. What Craig had said really resonated with him, even though for him it had been only a few months since his mom died.

"I guess I never thought of it that way before, Craig. That's interesting." Ben took a sip of his latte to give himself some time to process what Craig had said. "So, what did you do with all that anger you were feeling about your grandpa's death?"

"Well, that requires a little background, if you don't mind," Craig started and looked at Ben for permission.

"Yeah, for sure, please do," Ben replied.

"During that period of time I was referring to, a friend of mine invited me to go to church with him. As you no doubt remember, I wasn't much for organized religion at all back in the day.

"But I was in a place where I didn't really care, and I thought, What does it matter? I've got the time, and I wouldn't mind getting out of the house.

"When we got there, it was a pretty typical church service, but when the pastor got up and started talking about Jesus and the loss of his friend Lazarus, I was about ready to get up and walk out. Yet there was something about how he described the scene that caught my attention. His description of the interaction between him and Mary and Martha was nothing I had ever heard before. He painted it in such raw and human terms that I was gasping halfway through the message."

He paused to see if Ben was still following him. Finding that he was still engaged, Craig continued. "Like, for example, he talked about how when Martha heard that Jesus was coming, she charged out of the house and basically stuck her finger in Jesus' chest and said, "Where have you been?!" The thing about it, though, was that Jesus didn't get defensive or push back on Martha; he let her have her anger and frustration over what happened. I could really identify with that, but when I got angry over my grandpa's death, it seemed like all I got was Christian platitudes rather than people giving me the space to be angry like Jesus did for Martha. The long and the short of it was that something seized up in me, and I thought, *I want to know that Jesus.* So, I got up after the service was over and talked to the pastor. He was cool and easy to talk to. He asked me how my relationship with Jesus was, and I said I didn't have one. I just had never heard Jesus described that way at all, and I wanted to know more. He gave me his phone number and eventually we met and talked further about Jesus and how his portrayal by the church isn't all that accurate in light of our human tendencies. Over time, as I met with him, I began to see that Jesus was who He said He was, and He had proved it over and over again. Eventually, I made my own profession of faith in Jesus and have been doing all I can to develop a personal and even conversational relationship with Him."

Ben was stunned, and it took him completely off guard to hear Craig describe his experiences the way he did. It seemed to him that Craig was the last person who would become a

Christ follower, but here they were talking more about Jesus than Ben had in a long time. As a matter of fact, the story Craig told of Martha and Jesus really resonated with him too. Martha's anger at Jesus for not being there when she needed him, or even when her brother needed him, really struck a chord in Ben. He identified with that and with what appeared to him to be God's complete disengagement from his circumstances. Obviously, he needed to rethink his posture about that.

⸻ ∞ ⸻

During the spring of our grief we are hit with the return of painful emotions, and with those emotions come the memories, both good and bad. The challenge is not to shy away from either kind of memory. Those memories are us experiencing the "fabric" of our relationship with the person we have lost. One of the things to be mindful of is that we are always encoding memories, particularly in context with the person and even the surroundings. So when you walk into a room and get hit with a memory of the person you've lost, maybe next time just stop and allow the memory to run its course. We have a tendency to try to make those memories tangible, and that is what memorials are for. They root each memory in time and even place (e.g., standing at the graveside). Memorials are not the kind of thing we can take with us, but our memories will be always with us. Our memories are the melody of the music of relationship we had with our loved one. They are not only things that were said but the facial expressions they might have made or even their unique perfume or cologne. It's all part of the package of dynamic memories that are indelibly a part of our lives after they are gone. Our temptation is to condemn them because when they appear, we feel more pain, and we're sure that we've had enough. This reaction in us is quite understandable, but as this season progresses, there may come a time when you can give yourself permission to experience those memories once again.

17

PHANTOMS

*"When the river of emotions bursts its banks and expectations
go over the edges of reality, the brain creates hallucinations.
Anxiety-stricken people feel illusive vibrating alerts and hear
phantom phone rings, since absence of ringing generates scaring
emptiness and destroys their self-esteem."*

—Erik Pevernagie

Recently, Ben had decided to take the advice of Dr. Wheatley and his dad to join a men's grief group. In the weeks following the first meeting he attended, Ben found himself going about his days just like nothing really happened. There were fewer and fewer memory intrusions into his awareness about his mom. This may have been the level of distraction he had going in his life with his last year of school, the classes he was taking, and just keeping up with his part-time work schedule.

Occasionally, he would have to remind himself that his mom wasn't home anymore for him to talk to her. His dad was pretty consistent calling him on Sunday afternoons to check in on him and catch up with how life was going at school. During one of their calls, Ben's dad mentioned something that caught his attention.

"Hey, Ben, one last thing before I sign off."

"Sure, Dad, what's up?"

"Your sister has been making some comments now and again about wanting to talk to you, but she doesn't want to intrude on our phone call. Would you be willing to give her a call and just see how she's doing with your mom being gone? She's not giving me much to work with in terms of her thoughts and emotions about losing her mom. Maybe she'd talk to you."

"I'd be glad to do that, Dad. I'll give her a call later this week so it doesn't seem so obvious, how's that?" Ben wanted to avoid creating the impression with his sister that he was only doing his dad's bidding rather than being motivated by his love and concern for his sister.

"Sounds good, BK. Thanks for doing that. I'm worried about her." His dad's voice sounded weary and worried.

"No problem, Dad. You *do* know that I can only be a bridge between you two. There are things that only you can say that will help her. I know it may not feel that way, but given her age we are going to have to fight through the awkwardness we feel and her avoidance to push into the reality of what has happened." Ben wanted to remind his dad of something he'd just learned.

"Look at you! When did you get so smart?" His dad chuckled at the irony of his son giving him such sage advice.

His dad continued, "No, no, I know you're right. I'm not trying to get you to do my work for me. I just want someone in our family to be a point of contact for her for the time being. I'll work on taking a walk or something with her to see if I can pump the conversation handle to get some interaction going."

"What does that even mean, Dad? C'mon, you're going to have to update your phrases so the younger generation can follow what you're saying." Ben was laughing at the aphorisms and phrases his dad was known for. They usually prompted eye rolls from both himself and his sister, Christine.

"Oh c'mon, BK, you know what I mean, right?"

"Nope," Ben said.

"In days gone by, when dinosaurs roamed the earth, we used to have to pump a handle on the water pump to get water to flow out of it. If you were going to have water continuously, then you'd have to keep pumping!" Now his dad was laughing at his son's ignorance. He detected in Ben's voice the eye roll happening, as it always did.

"Okay, okay, now I get it. Thanks for the explanation. Oh brother, really, Dad?"

"Well, on that note, I'm going to sign off and get back to creating more irritating dad jokes. Good talking to you, son! I hope your week is a good one, and I'll talk to you next Sunday."

"See ya, Dad! Thanks for calling." Ben hit the end button on his phone and went back to getting ready for the week.

A few days later, Ben dialed his sister's cell phone number.

"Hello?" Christine answered, but it was distinctly flat in tone and even enthusiasm. She was clearly not okay. In times past, when Ben called, his sister would often greet him with "Hey, big brother! How's my hero?" He would tell her to shut up, and then the conversation would be off to a roaring start. This time was muted, to say the least.

"Hey, little sister, how's it going?" He tried to sound as natural as he knew how, but the concern was already growing in him.

"I'm okay," she replied flatly. "Do you have any idea how long it's been that Mom has been gone?" There was an edge to her voice that sounded familiar to him.

"Sure I do, Christine. It's been four months. Why?" It wasn't like he had to think about it. He had been marking time, too, since his mom died.

"You know, it's been the longest four months of my life. It seems like every day is filled with reminders of Mom. I just can't get away from them. It's just too much, BK. I can't keep doing this." Her voice trailed off into a stream of tears.

Ben's heart broke for his sister. At that moment in time he really wished he could be home and put his arm around her. He felt so helpless.

"I'm not sure what to say, Chris," he started hesitantly. "I'm trying to avoid doing what everyone seems to be doing to both of us, saying something trite or comforting when there is no comfort to be found."

As he was finishing his sentence, he could hear his sister's breathing quickening. He had the distinct impression that she was moving from sadness to fury.

"You're damn right there is nothing to say! MOM IS GONE AND SHE IS NOT COMING BACK! I'm so pissed I can't even sleep or speak!" It seemed to Ben that his sister had been waiting for an opportunity to safely explode somewhere, and he was thankful it was with him.

She continued, "THIS IS UNIMAGINABLE, BK! IT JUST FEELS SO EMPTY AND SILENT."

She slowed down, and her voice quieted to a strained whisper. "Mom would make sounds around the house. Sometimes she'd talk to herself as she was working on a project, or she would have some music playing. You remember, BK?"

"Yeah, I remember, Chris. You could always find her in the house because of those sounds she would make. It was annoying and even a little intrusive if you were anywhere nearby, but now it all seems different. Now you just want to hear it again no matter how irritating it might be." His voice trailed off into memories as he recalled one time being in his room trying to write a paper when his mom was cleaning out a closet nearby. He had to get his headphones out just to tune out the ongoing cacophony of verbalized thoughts, self-instructions, and declarations.

"Yes exactly," replied Chris. "The creepy thing is that there are times where I swear I'm hearing them again. I know that she's gone, but I find that I have to remind myself that she is gone, and those sounds can't be her."

———— ◦❀◦ ————

Phantom experiences are not uncommon in our recovery from our grief. As the quote at the beginning of this chapter points out, we get accustomed to a variety of things connected to the person we love. It takes very little to trigger these associations, and that's what we often refer to as phantom experiences. It is an important part of our grieving process to slowly detach from these associations that were made over time with the person we've lost. This includes the sounds that Ben and Chris were talking about but also smells or routines around the house. So, just remember, it's a normal part of your grieving experience, and be careful to avoid turning it into something dramatically pathological. The reality is that it is profoundly human to have these kinds of experiences. Affirm for yourself that it is normal and to be expected, and don't fall into the shame spiral thinking there is something dramatically wrong with you. If anything, what you are experiencing is very human.

18

THIS IS HARDER THAN
I THOUGHT

"I think this is when most people give up on their stories. . . .
[They] get into the middle and discover it was harder than they
thought. They can't see the distant shore anymore, and they
wonder if their paddling is moving them forward. None of
the trees behind them are getting smaller and none of the trees
ahead are getting bigger. They take it out on their spouses, and
they go looking for an easier story."
—Donald Miller

Ben had just finished his class and was walking past a
bulletin board he had seen dozens of time. There was
a new flyer that he hadn't noticed before, so he stopped to
check it out. The flyer was inviting students to get involved
in a group who worked with cancer survivors and their family
members at the local hospital. Ben thought, *Maybe doing*
something like this would help me along in processing my grief.
It's a good fit with my experiences and what these family members
are experiencing.

He took down the necessary contact information, and
when he got back to his apartment, he emailed the contact
person. It was only a few hours later that he got an email from
a senior psych major named Emma. She invited him to check
things out at the information meeting coming up in a couple
of days. The day rolled around, and Ben found out that the

group went to the hospital a couple of times a month to help cancer patients with whatever they needed, including child care, running errands for caregivers, and just hanging out to pass the long days in the hospital. Ben felt like it was a good fit for his schedule and his continuing need to stay engaged in his grief. He knew that it was probably going to be hard, but he thought he would be up for it.

When the day came, the volunteer group met at the hospital, and after Emma got them registered with the hospital staff, they took the elevator up to the unit. As they exited the elevator, Ben felt the memories flooding back of when his mom was in the hospital and he would go to visit her. Emma had taken care of all the arrangements regarding which families they were visiting. Ben was teamed up with Abby, who had lost her mom to a car accident.

As Ben and Abby visited with the family and the patient, they took the time to hear their stories. The family had an eight-year-old and a twelve-year-old. The dad of the family asked if Ben and Abby could take the kids out to the courtyard where they could feel the fresh air and talk to someone other than him. When they got down to the courtyard, Abby sat with the eight-year-old girl whose name was Liz, and Ben sat with the twelve-year-old boy, Jack. Thankfully, they had come prepared with games and other activities that would be a fun distraction for the kids.

Ben and Jack found a quiet bench away from Abby and Liz.

"So, Jack, what's the story with your mom?" Ben initiated the conversation.

"I don't know exactly, but my dad said that mom had cancer in her pan . . . pan . . . shoot, I can never pronounce it right." Jack stumbled over his words.

"It's okay, Jack, don't sweat it. Some of those medical terms are tough to pronounce for sure. You mean, pancreas?" Ben offered.

"Yeah, yeah, that's it!" Jack brightened a little. "Anyway, we were told about a month ago, and the doctor said she was going to need treatment soon in order to live longer."

"Wow, that's some tough news, Jack. How are you handling all this?" Ben pushed a little further.

"I try not to think about it, but my dad looks pretty worried when he looks at my mom." Jack looked over at a tree in the courtyard that had attracted a noisy bird who seemed compelled to be the soundtrack for their conversation.

"You know, Jack, I was once in your shoes not all that long ago," Ben revealed.

"Really?" Jack looked back at him.

"Yup," Ben replied. "My mom was in the hospital for a long time with a different kind of cancer than your mom, but these days in the hospital just seem to drag on forever."

"Yeah, for sure. So, Ben, what happened with your mom? Did she get better?" Jack asked with a tone of hope in his voice.

"The first couple of times in the hospital, she would go home and did pretty well for a while, but then she ended up back in the hospital again." Ben feared where this line of questioning was going with Jack.

Ben he continued, "But then there was the last time where she just couldn't beat it, and we all had to say good-bye. It was really tough.

"Listen, you guys don't seem like you are to that stage just yet, so the key is to enjoy the day that you have as much as you can. Those are the days you will remember." Ben smiled at Jack and patted him on the shoulder.

Ben and Jack wrapped up their conversation and were both amazed that they didn't have time to play a game or something else.

As Ben and Abby were driving home, Ben was reflecting on his time with Jack.

"So, Abby, how did it go with Liz?" Ben asked.

"Oh fine," Abby replied. "She was a regular chatterbox about her life in third grade and her friends back home that she doesn't get to see as much she would like. How was your time with Jack?"

"Quite honestly, it was harder than I thought. I mean, talking to him wasn't that hard, but it was fighting off all the memories of my own. For some reason, I thought this would be easier since I'm talking to someone else, especially given the fact that it's been a good six months since my mom died."

———— ∞ ————

One of the greatest obstacles are our unrealistic expectations about the length of time it takes to recover from our grief. As a matter of fact, it's not really an expectation that we have at all but our wish or hope that it will be over soon. Our expectations often reflect our familiarity with a given situation (in this case our grief) and a reasonable guess of what is supposed to happen. Our hopes, on the other hand, are a form of wishful thinking about the ideal reality we desire to see happen. It's completely normal to hope for a positive outcome, but we have to find a way to calibrate how we are living with the realities of life that we are experiencing. That doesn't mean just resigning ourselves to the grief never ending, but it also doesn't mean getting disappointed when it's not over when we think it *should* be.

I realize this is a tall order because making our grief easier, shorter, or less painful is our preferred outcome, but there are variables to our grieving that are often hidden to us that don't reveal themselves until we hit the summer of our grief. It's during this time as we try to move back into life that there are some glaring holes left behind from the person's absence. Our challenge is to recognize those holes, allow ourselves to feel the loss (again), but continue the journey into new relationships. You will often feel a certain ambivalence about moving forward, but what has been developed over the course of your journey until now is an ability to weather the waves of fear, anger, sadness, resignation, and acceptance. The difference is that by this time, you've developed some skill and perspective in managing these emotions. Withstand the waves, and keep wading out into new skills and relationships!

19

LEVERAGING MY PAIN

"Pain is inevitable; suffering is optional."
—Buddhist proverb

After what happened in the visit to the local hospital, Ben decided to go back to his men's grief group for a check-in to assess how he was doing in his grief recovery. There were a few new members in the group since he had been there last, which was over a month ago. One of them was a younger guy, Caleb, who had lost his wife to breast cancer.

They went around as they usually did to get a quick check-in to see how everyone was doing, and to get an idea who needed some time to talk. Caleb indicated that he could use some time to think through something with the group. It was Ben's turn, and he said he was there to do a check-up with his grief journey but was content to listen as the other guys each had their opportunity to speak.

Caleb started and indicated that the last month or so had been really tough. What he had found was that it was hard for him to be honest about the amount of pain he was feeling. He had two small kids at home, and he just couldn't find anywhere to unravel his thoughts.

"What I'm struggling with is the pain I feel about Sasha being gone. The last few months of her hospitalization were really difficult. It seemed like all I could do was stand there and watch her waste away." Caleb had started talking to the group, but by the time he was done, he was staring at the floor. "I just felt so helpless."

"So, just to be clear," Nate responded, "you had expected it not to be so difficult?"

"Yeah, kinda," he said. "It's hard to admit, but I was relieved when she finally died because she was out of the pain finally." Tears were forming in his eyes. "I mean, it's pretty clear that her pain is over, but mine is still a constant companion. I think I would be able to handle it if I thought I could grasp what Paul talks about in Romans when he says, 'And we know that for those who love God all things work together for good, for those who are called according to his purpose.'"

As the conversation continued between Caleb and other group members, Ben found himself getting more and more irritated. It just seemed to him that Caleb wasn't being honest about how God works in the midst of our struggle and pain. Ben didn't think it was quite that easy. At least he hadn't found it to be that way.

Caleb continued, "At least at this point in the journey, I've got to believe that this pain I am feeling will benefit someone in the future."

Ben couldn't hold back. "Woah, woah Caleb. I'm wondering not so much about the benefit to others, but the benefit to you. This sounds a little like you're saying that somehow what we are experiencing is a good thing! In what universe is this kind of pain a good thing for anyone?" Ben was trying to hold it back, but it seeped out through his sarcasm.

"That's fair, I suppose," Caleb began. "I just don't think that I'm going to know at this point what is the benefit to me. Right now, I don't see any at all, and the road ahead is still pretty blurry."

Nate interjected, "Okay, slow down a bit, Ben. I don't hear Caleb emphasizing one person over himself. The bigger picture is that if we had a better idea what perspective was needed, it might give us the motivation to continue down this path. I would remind everyone that not all pain is bad, and statements like that about pain are actually pretty oversimplified and don't describe the process of recovery very accurately."

Caleb was nodding. "Yeah, I guess I'm not making myself very clear. In no way would I say that pain is a good thing, particularly when it comes to losing someone you love. What I *am* saying is that some perspective about the benefit this pain will provide others around me, or even about me going forward without Sasha, would be helpful to sustain my motivation to keep working the process. That's all."

Ben's frustration calmed down a bit. Through his own process it had been hard to deal with people's platitudes, which oversimplified the reality he was living with *his* pain.

"I guess I hadn't thought that my experiences and learning would benefit anyone but me," Ben said. "That verse in Romans has always stuck in my craw every time someone brings it up because it seems to diminish the gravity of the moment the person, specifically me in this case, is in. I don't mean you specifically, Caleb. I've been walking this path for long enough that I'm not sure there's anything I haven't heard, including innumerable Bible verses that are meant to encourage but end up discouraging and even shaming the person for their unwillingness to 'see the good' in their trial. What I have found is the person hasn't earned the right to speak into my life like that."

"Good point, Ben," Nate jumped in. "No matter whether we are only days away from our loss or years, it seems that there is no end to the well-meaning people who will speak these platitudes without knowing the actual damage they cause."

We will often confront people in our lives who are truly trying to help but just can't seem to enter into our pain without trying to spout a platitude. At the same time, Caleb had a point about our pain, particularly at this season of our grief. There is an important process here as we move further and further away from the initial loss, and that is to revisit our conclusions about the pain of our loss. Not to paste over with happy, but to begin the process of placing it into some perspective. That perspective can change over time. For example, I could not say that the loss of my dad was a good thing for a long, long time. Of course, I resisted processing it at all for a decade or so, but when I started the grief work I needed to do, way down the road, I began to see what the impact of my dad's death was on me. Eventually, it turned into writing a book and teaching courses on grief and loss. Now the things that I would have bristled over closer to my loss, I can now see how they have been leveraged for my growth and others' encouragement. There is no way that we can impose that perspective on the days, weeks, and months after the initial shock of loss. That would be engaging in the kind of denial that we talked about during the winter season. Perspective and meaning from our loss is meant to age with us. The only requirement is that we keep our eyes open for opportunities to grow and come alongside others.

20

"The Path of Suffering"

*"Twice in that life, I've been given the choice: as a boy
and as a man. The boy chose safety, the man chooses suffering.
The pain now is part of the happiness then. That's the deal."*
—C.S. Lewis

During the class Ben was going to with his friend Tony, the professor talked about how important journaling could be in grieving well. When he heard that, he thought that it was a great idea but not for him. He didn't have time to do something like that in spite of the fact that he had no idea how long it would actually take. He felt that the men's group was more than enough in terms of heart exploration. He didn't need any more. The truth of the matter was that he didn't want to look at the walls of his prison cell. He had talked to Nate about it but hadn't done much about it. He was safe, secure, and less vulnerable, and that was the point. This prison cell was his guarantee that no more damage would occur in his relationships with people or even in his relationship with himself. He just wasn't willing to take the risk.

Just as he was getting comfortable with this arrangement of safety and invulnerability with his cell, and really having no one in his world who would challenge his handling of his emotions, he got an email from Nate inviting him to a group showing of the movie *Shadowlands*. Ben had never heard of it, and he went into it skeptical that it would have anything to do with him.

The day came, and Ben had nothing else to do, so he went to Nate's apartment, which was across the apartment complex from his. Nate answered the door and invited him in. All the guys were there, and it didn't take long for the movie to get started.

It was when Joy Grisham was diagnosed with cancer that his defenses began to collapse. It was the first moment in the movie when the story brushed a little too close to the story of his mom's cancer. Her prognosis was anywhere from weeks to months.

At one point in the movie, Joy initiated a conversation about the future. This conversation was just like a conversation Ben had had with his mom during her last days. It was seared into his memory.

"Ben, we need to talk about the future." Her breathing was like she was out of breath from climbing a flight of stairs. She took a few deep breaths of the oxygen from the tubes entering her nose.

"Nah, let's not talk about that now, Mom." Ben looked down trying to think of a way to get his mom off this track. He *really* didn't want to talk about this.

"No, we need to talk about it because the reality of this is coming. I wouldn't be your mom without thinking about this, and I love you and want you to walk into life without me." She was working hard to stay in the conversation in spite of the distracting pain that she was in.

"Mom, just stop! You can barely breathe. Just chill, and let's deal with this later." He was buying time in spite of the fact that he knew his mom was not going to let it go.

His comment seemed to focus her even more. "You don't tell your mother to chill! I'm not one of your buddies. Just listen to me, please?"

"Okay, okay, sorry," Ben responded, feeling like he had unnecessarily irritated his mom.

His mom smiled weakly and gathered her strength as she formed her sentence.

"Ben, I know how hard this must be for you and Dad and Christine. But I want you to remember what I say because we may not have another opportunity for this conversation. I want you to grieve when I'm gone. I would expect nothing else. I love you more than words can convey, and you have to know that leaving you breaks my heart too. But I want you to take your time in grieving and allow yourself to feel. It's more important for you than it is for me. I will be okay in the arms of Jesus, but you will have the hard job of walking through life without your mom." She paused, weighing her words.

Ben looked at his mom trying to soak in all that he was seeing and feeling. Tears rolled down his cheeks, and even if he wanted to, he couldn't get words out at all.

"Just rest, Mom. I love you too, and thanks for that. I will cherish it as long as I live." Ben gave her a hug, then left the room wiping away the tears as he left.

Just as he was coming back to the movie, he heard C.S. (Jack) Lewis reflect on his own life. He ends the movie with, "Twice in that life, I've been given the choice: as a boy and as a man. The boy chose safety, the man chooses suffering. The pain now is part of the happiness then. That's the deal." At that moment, everything came into focus, and Ben didn't exactly know what to do about it.

As we walk this journey of grief, we are confronted with a variety of choices, as suggested by the quote above, in terms of whether we will choose the safe road of avoiding anything that might be difficult or painful or whether we will choose the path of suffering. Doesn't sound very appealing to be sure, but it's important to define the suffering we are talking about. Often when we hear the word *suffering*, we think of the extreme end of what suffering would be like—terminal cancer, or dementia, or any number of maladies that could afflict us. Yet suffering has a far more common meaning than that, and it is individually defined for each person. Our temptation is to fall into comparing our experiences with someone else's. This comparison is usually in the service of giving us a good reason to avoid the grief that we feel.

The thing we have to keep in mind is that the suffering Jack is referring to is the plight of *every* human. It is the suffering of living in a broken world with a broken body in the context of broken people. Grief has an uncanny way of revealing the important things in our lives that we need to pay attention to. It also reveals things about us as well. Perhaps the suffering we face is the plight of being human and investing in relationships that we might lose in the future. As Lewis so aptly puts it, "That's the deal." If we choose the path of suffering, we choose the path of living the fullness of our humanity. It is in the contrast, the one between joy and sorrow, that we can actually find the depth and meaning our hearts long for. With that in mind, it is little wonder that King David can write both psalms of lament and sorrow as well as heartfelt psalms of joy, praise, and gratitude.

21

THE IMPORTANCE OF YOUR HEART

"Your vision will become clear only when you can look into your own heart. Who looks outside, dreams; who looks inside, awakes."

—Carl Jung

The more Ben listened to his professor, something was gnawing at him. The more his professor talked about the importance of our hearts, the more confused he became. Isn't our heart just the seat of our emotions? He understood the connection of the heart in dealing with all the emotions that were associated with grief, but why such an emphasis on all these other areas of our lives? Ben stopped by the podium after class and asked if he could make an appointment to meet with his professor. He had never done that before, so he was in uncharted territory when it came to how to address his questions, but he figured it was worth a shot.

The professor was welcoming and kind, and invited Ben to meet with him at two o'clock on Wednesday afternoon. It just so happened that Ben's class schedule allowed that, so he accepted and left the class a little apprehensive, but he found himself looking forward to this meeting.

When Wednesday came around, Ben headed over after his last class to his professor's office. Soon the professor came out and greeted him, and they walked back to his office.

Instead of sitting in front of his desk, like most profs, he had a couple of chairs in his office that faced one another. When Ben noticed this, he was a little unnerved, but he entered and waited to be instructed where to sit.

"Good to have you, Ben! Go ahead and take a seat" His professor gestured to one of the chairs. Ben sat and was surprised when the professor moved over into the chair facing him.

"So, what's on your mind, Ben?" the professor asked.

"I don't know, Dr. Salter. I guess I'm just a little confused about all that you're saying about our hearts. I get the role that our hearts play in the grieving process, but from the sound of it, you seem to think it's much more than that. Can you help me understand that a little better?"

"Sure, I'd be glad to. Before I do, though, would you bring me up to speed with your story and how the class is impacting you?"

"Yeah, sure," Ben started. "About six months ago my mom died of breast cancer. It was a pretty devastating blow to my family and to me. Since then I've had the opportunity to be in a grief group for men."

"Which is a relative rarity," his professor interjected.

"Yeah, it's been a great group, and I've learned a lot about my own journey and about the other guys who are going through something similar. I found it ironic that I was going to be taking your class this fall. I've heard a lot about it, but since I'm a business major, I haven't had much occasion to take a psychology class at all. But since it's my senior year and I had a few electives to fill, I thought it might be a good idea."

"I hear that a lot, Ben, and I'm grateful that you took the chance to take this class. So just one more question. How has the loss of your mom been impacting you since you've been back at school?"

"It's on again, off again, if you know what I mean. Some days are really hard, and I particularly feel the pain of not being able to call my mom and check in with her, and others it's almost like nothing has happened. Those days I struggle with guilt about not feeling anything. I mean, isn't someone who is grieving feeling it all the time, and if you don't, does it mean that you're forgetting the person?"

Dr. Salter smiled knowingly. "Those stereotypes sure come back to bite us, don't they? Generally, I would say that your experience sounds pretty normal.

"Now, to your question about our hearts. I guess I take my inspiration for all my talk about our hearts from Proverbs 4:23, which says, 'Keep your heart with all vigilance, for from it flow the springs of life.' In Scripture, the heart is not only the seat of emotion but actually the 'seat' of everything about us. It includes our dreams, our hopes, and decisions, *and* our emotions. Notice what that verse said: 'For from it flow the springs of life.' Right? Often times springs were turned into wells that everyone could benefit from. Our hearts are the well of our lives, and from it flows life, or, not to be dramatic, separation from God. So, when I say our hearts are the core of who we are, vitally important to our journey through grief, I mean to say that we need to bring *all* of us into the journey, not just our thoughts and decisions, but all of us."

Professor Salter paused to see if Ben was following him. "You see what I mean?"

"Yep, I do. That makes so much more sense now. I do appreciate you explaining that to me, and I can also see the role of our heart in the grieving process since there is a hole left behind in it when someone important to us dies."

"Exactly, Ben! Now, let me shift the metaphor for a hot minute. Imagine for a brief time that you were to look at your heart as a landscape or a plot of ground. What would it look like, Ben? Let me explain why I ask that. Many years ago, when I was navigating my own grief journey, I felt like my heart was just a desert. There was nothing growing there, nothing interesting about it, and it was something that only got in the way of functioning effectively. Not only that, but there was one area of the landscape of my heart that was cordoned off from anyone venturing in there, and that was all my memories, feelings, and thoughts about my dad whom I'd lost as a kid of only twelve years old. I didn't want anyone in there because it was such a mess of emotions and everything else that it was easier to just never visit there. You get the idea?" He looked expectantly at Ben.

"Yes, absolutely. That makes perfect sense, Dr. Salter. So I bet you're wondering what the landscape of my heart looks like?"

His professor nodded.

"Well, actually there are wide swaths of emotions and conclusions that are completely walled off from me experiencing them. It seems that whenever I'm around other people who are grieving, I don't go into that area, it's kind of like a no-go zone. I work only on being helpful and supportive, but my story is safely behind the wall where no one can know or see it. I believe that part of my landscape, as you call it, is only painful, and I've decided to let it be."

"Yes, I hear you, Ben. What if today I could convince you that it is out of those places that your ability to connect and be present with people is very, very important?"

It is a good practice to walk the landscape of our own hearts as we consider the impact our loss has had on us. There are a myriad of thoughts and conclusions about your internal world, the external world, and the God you may have worshiped and now have abandoned out of anger and sadness. Initially, our landscape can look pretty bleak without a lot of color in it. But it is critical to incorporate our own stories into our own experiences. That is an important part of the summer of our grief. We need to integrate what we have been through into a narrative of our relationship with the person lost, but also our relationship with everyone else and God.

22

THE HOUSE OF MOURNING

"The timing of death, like the ending of a story, gives a changed meaning to what preceded it."
—Mary Catherine Bateson, author

"Hey, Ben! How's it going?" Greg had become a good friend during the time Ben was participating in the men's group. They had met a couple of times for coffee and had good conversations about life and their shared experience with grief.

"Good, good, Greg! How are you doing?" Ben was genuinely happy to see Greg. He was feeling something he hadn't felt in quite a while: a sense of familiarity and friendship. This had been absent in his life up to this season of his grief.

Ben took a seat next to Greg as the other members of the group gathered and got comfortable. As a group, their usual routine was to check in with each group member to see how he was doing, and if anyone needed some time to talk about something, he would indicate it then.

It was Ben's turn. "Things seem to be going pretty well. It's the first time in a while that I've felt pretty solid. That certainly hasn't been the case before, and in some ways it feels like I'm turning some kind of corner with my grief. I'm not running, distracting, minimizing, or obsessing about it. I think it's fair to say that I'm getting closer to acceptance than I have been in quite some time. So, I guess I'm feeling encouraged tonight."

Greg went next. "I've been reading something in the book of Ecclesiastes that has really gotten me thinking. Actually it's pretty jarring, but other than that, I'm feeling pretty good. I think I would like some time to think it through with you guys and see what you think."

Three more members of the group and the group leader, Nate, did their check-ins. Once that was completed, Nate turned to Greg. "So, Greg . . . you piqued my curiosity about what you were reading in Ecclesiastes. You wanna lead us out?"

"Sure, " Greg replied. "So I heard a sermon by our pastor last weekend, and he was looking at what's called the book of wisdom in the Bible called Ecclesiastes. Do you mind if I read from it, Nate?"

"No, not at all, Greg. Go right ahead," Nate responded, grinning like he knew what was coming.

Greg pulled out his phone, found the place in Scripture he was looking for, and began to read. "It is better to go to the house of mourning than to go to the house of feasting, for this is the end of all mankind, and the living will lay it to heart. Sorrow is better than laughter, for by sadness of face the heart is made glad. The heart of the wise is in the house of mourning, but the heart of fools is in the house of mirth."

Nate interjected, "Greg, where is that in Ecclesiastes for those of us who would like to follow along?"

"It's in Ecclesiastes 7, verses two through four," Greg answered.

He continued, "I guess the thing that has been annoying me is that the teacher, which is what he is called in the book, makes it sound like the house of mourning is a good thing. I mean, how in the world can he say, 'Sorrow is better than laughter for by sadness the heart is made glad'? That's insane! Until I heard some thoughts from my pastor about it. I'm still not sure how mourning can be something good, but the pastor pointed out that the house of mourning is better than a party because, if allowed, it will prompt people who develop the wisdom to consider reality as it is and not as they would have it. I've always considered wise people as having enough experience to provide clarity to live by for people who are just getting started. I never really accounted for mourning and grief as part of that."

Jim, a relatively new member of the group, was particularly outspoken when spiritual things were brought up. His tendency in his responses was to diminish and even belittle such beliefs as traditions and superstitions. He was the next to respond. "Yeah, I'm with you, Greg. That doesn't make sense at all. It seems to me that I'm flush with enough reality. I don't see any reason to go looking for it."

Nate spoke up. "That might be so, Jim, but as we all recall about the seasons of our grief, there is an ongoing effort to accept reality that looks a little different with each passing season and therefore is a continual part of the grieving process."

"Yeah, I certainly understand where you are coming from, Jim," Greg responded, "but I have heard it said that grief has a way of revealing things about us and how we think and feel that would otherwise be hidden to us without it. The conclusion I came up with after thinking it through is that wisdom is found not only in the positive experiences we have had but also in the 'valley' experiences that we walk through . . . like grief and loss. It seems to me that either I can lean into my grief or I can run away from it into the distractions and numbing behaviors I have certainly tried. I guess I never thought that the people in my life who are the most helpful have been through valleys in their lives, whether with grief or not. Those valleys have helped them to develop a perspective about life and living that is considered 'wisdom' out here to us who are just getting going on the journey."

Ben wouldn't have considered himself a very religious person, but when Greg explained that, he had a newfound interest and curiosity about the book Greg was talking about. He could use that kind of wisdom in his life, to be sure. He realized that he had concluded that mourning and grief were just life-disrupting processes to get through, not something to learn from. During this summer of grief, Ben had to reorient (again) his thinking to include his grief and sorrow as a vital part of his story, not just a parenthetical part of his story. He realized that he was much more willing to do that now than he had been just a few months ago. The other thing that he was getting accustomed to was that his mom was now a part of his story rather than an active participant in it. That also meant that in spite of the fact that she wasn't actively participating in it now, her fingerprints were all over his life and story. He wouldn't have been the man he was without her. At that moment in time, Ben felt both sadness and gratitude all at once.

———✧———

As you can tell, Ben's story is changing even within the seasons he has experienced so far. One of the areas that is critical to engage with and not withdraw from is allowing your story to be rewritten so that your lost loved one can begin to recede into the background. Allowing this to happen is not to forget, or deny, or minimize, but to create space in your heart for the person to continue living even though he or she is gone physically.

23

THE LESSON OF CYCLES

"Humans like to consider everything as linear,
when in reality everything is cyclic."
—Robert Black

Joy was enjoying her cup of coffee on the front porch when her phone buzzed. She picked it up to see who it was, and saw that it was Lauren from her fateful lunch a few weeks back.

"Hey, Lauren!" Joy answered cautiously. "What's up?"

"Hi, Joy! I wanted to check in after our lunch a few weeks ago. I was a little worried about you. You left in quite a hurry."

"Yeah, to be really honest it was pretty painful to have those platitudes thrown at me. Quite honestly, it was pretty invalidating. I realize that you weren't part of the platitude crowd, but it seemed a little odd that you didn't speak up. I certainly understood why you didn't in light of the circumstances."

"Well, that's pretty gracious of you, Joy. I do appreciate it. But that's why I called. I was wondering if you wanted to get coffee somewhere between you and me, just the two of us?" Joy could tell Lauren was being careful in how she worded her request.

"Yeah, I would be up for that as long as it's just you and me," Joy responded.

"Okay, how about Common Grounds? I think that is about the middle between us."

"Sure, that's a great place," Joy answered. "How about one p.m.?"

"That'll work. See you then!"

It was a few days before they would meet, so Joy had some time to get herself ready for another attempt at relationships. This time she hoped she would have better luck than the last time. Her friendship with Lauren goes all the way back to their freshman year in college when they met each other in an Intro to Psychology class. They got to be pretty good friends over the three years of school they shared. Joy had to cut hers short because of her pregnancy, so she did the rest of her college classes online, and that was when she fell further and further out of touch with her friends like Lauren.

Joy arrived at the coffee shop before Lauren to get a decent table and to get her head in a place to try this conversation again. Lauren arrived about fifteen minutes later. Lauren waved as she came in, ordered her drink, and joined Joy at the table.

"Hi, Joy! Thanks so much for meeting with me. After the debacle of the last meeting, I would have understood completely if you had said no." She smiled knowingly.

"Really? You mean you saw what was happening during that lunch? I thought I was the only one, and it made me feel like I did something wrong when I was trying to recover from losing Aaron."

"Oh, Joy, I have to apologize for not stepping in and shutting that crap down. They are just so dismissive when they say stuff like that, and I'm sorry I didn't." There was genuine remorse in Lauren's expression. So much so that it moved Joy to know that a friend would feel so deeply for what she was feeling.

"I really do appreciate you saying so, Lauren. It's times like those that people going through grief feel that much more alone," Joy replied.

"If you don't mind, though, may I explain what my silence was about? I realize this doesn't excuse what I didn't do, but it might give you a little context," Lauren said.

"Of course, Lauren. I would love that." Joy smiled in relief that perhaps she had found someone who understood a little of what she felt and what she was going through.

"About a year ago my Mimi—that's what we called my grandmother—died. My Paps, my grandfather, asked me if I would be willing to come and live with them for a time to help Mimi get around and just hang out with her since her days could get pretty long being in bed most of the time." Lauren paused, walking back through the memories. "It was some of the most memorable days and weeks I spent with her. We played card games, she sang some of her favorite hymns to me, and we just reminisced about when I was a little girl and how much she enjoyed being a part of my life. But at one point something happened and she wasn't able to recall things. The hardest was that at first she didn't know my name, and eventually she didn't recognize me at all." Lauren sighed and took in a deep breath as she fought back the tears.

"Wow, that must have been so hard, Lauren. I'm so sorry!" Joy responded and reached out to touch Lauren's hand.

"Yeah, well, that was when it got really hard to take care of her because I was like a stranger to her and she didn't trust anyone, including me. I kept telling myself it was the disease that was stealing away my Mimi, but it didn't make much difference when to her I was a stranger, and to me she was my grandmother that I loved dearly."

"Wow, that must have been really tough, Lauren. Ugh"

Lauren took a deep breath and continued, "When she finally passed away, I was by her side when we said good-bye to her. I don't think I will ever forget that day.

"The aftermath of all that is that the friend group that I was a part of, the one that met with you a few weeks ago, did all they could to support and comfort me, but all they could generate were the same platitudes they threw at you. 'Time heals all wounds,' or 'At least she's in a better place now,' or my favorite, 'She's watching over you now.' I got so mad, I couldn't even speak to them. Our lunch with them was really the first time I hung out with them for any length of time. So, when they started in on you, I just froze. It was like I was back there again." Lauren looked up from her coffee with tears in her eyes.

"I regret that I didn't protect you, not to mention the fact that it probably would have done me good to speak up and protect my own heart against such attacks. I do get it, Joy."

"Well, thanks, Lauren. I'm happy to hear that I'm not alone feeling the way I did. I probably could have done a better job communicating how much it hurt, but with people like that I wonder if you are only inviting more statements like the ones they're saying."

"Yeah, I suppose that is true," Lauren replied.

"Something that I have found out, in this relatively short but grueling journey through grief, is that on the path we have chosen, the path of healing from our grief, a lot of people will not appreciate or even support us even though their words say they do. It is just a hard reality to accept, and sometimes I go so far as to ask my mom, 'Can't we just skip to the happy part again?'"

They both laughed at Joy's request to her mom, not in an effort to dismiss it but recognizing how true it was for both of them.

As Joy walked away and drove home, she was proud of herself for keeping her voice and protecting her own heart. It was comforting to find someone like Lauren who would truly support her in real time, not with pleasant platitudes or simple solutions.

—— ⚭ ——

During the summer season of our grief, there is an ongoing cycle of denial and acceptance that occurs, as we see in Joy's description to her friend Lauren. When the denial kicks in, we have some measure of relief from all the feelings that have awakened during the spring, but then there is a moment of reckoning, like Joy felt with her friends that demanded her either to go back into denial or to work to accept the reality she was living in without any comparison to anyone else's experience. It takes key people in our lives to encourage us to face it head-on and keep trudging through. It doesn't have to be pretty; we just have to be consistent and committed to healing from such a profound loss.

24

WRESTLING WITH GUILT OR SHAME?

"I get up and pace the room, as if I can leave my guilt behind me. But it tracks me as I walk, an ugly shadow made by myself."
—Sister Rosamund Lupton

Joy had the weekend off from her work at the library, so she slept in, got up, poured a cup of coffee, and took a stroll around the neighborhood. The kind of stroll that was slow enough not only for her to take in the surroundings, even though it was starting to get hot, but also to reflect on what had happened over the last few months. She had stumbled her way through the winter of her grief, fighting to accept the reality of Aaron's death, into the reawakening of her feelings in the spring, and here she was facing the summer—not only physically, but emotionally—and asking herself, *Where do I go from here?*

She turned a corner and passed a couple with a baby in a stroller, and she instantly felt the pain she always felt when this happened. *Is this ever going to stop? What is wrong with me that I can't let go of all the "should haves" when it comes to Aaron? I should be past this by now so I can look at a couple and not feel the stab of pain that I always do!*

The moment that thought took hold, her internal recording hit play and took off at breakneck speed. I should have gone to the doctor earlier. If only I had called the doctor and insisted that he do an ultrasound. Maybe this was punishment for what I did with Caleb. There was a slew of thoughts that were entirely focused on what she could have done—and the additional weight of what she didn't think to do. In other words, she was guilty of what she did do, and she was guilty of what she didn't do.

Soon her thoughts took a leap from those doubts to the kind of person she was. You couldn't have been a good mom anyway because of who you are! What kind of person would ignore the obvious signs that her baby was in distress? It's just further proof that you don't deserve anything good. You're just a loser and will always be a loser. You should have known better. How could you have missed the signs of how Caleb was treating you? You're weak for not getting out of that relationship before all this happened.

Joy was shaking her head and listening attentively all at the same time, both figuratively and literally, if that was even possible. As she continued her walk, it felt like a huge, cold, wet weighted blanket had descended upon her shoulders. Instead of looking up to see where she was going, all she could do was watch her feet and the sidewalk. The next time she looked up, she was at her house, and she climbed wearily up the steps as if she had been speed-walking a marathon.

She plopped down on one of the chairs on the front porch. She left her stuff there and went into the house to get her journal. When she came back out to sit down, she opened her journal and realized she hadn't written anything for at least a month.

She put her pen to paper.

This walk that I have taken today has been anything but relaxing and reflective like I had hoped. It feels like

I am in the middle of a wrestling match with both guilt and shame. At this point in the match, I feel like I am holding my own, but guilt and shame have some pretty potent weapons in the "if only" and "you should have" kind of statements.

Are there things I could have done? Yes, of course. So there is some element in truth in that, but at the same time, how could I have known? No one told me or warned me about the possibility of stillbirth and what the signs might have been. It's pretty clear to me that I'm feeling pretty out of control right now, and that is what is giving fuel to these statements. I may not be able to control what happened, but I may be able to rewrite what happened by changing reality enough to make it all come out the way it should have. And then there's the shame that would have me believe that the reason things came out the way that they did was because I'm such a flawed person, there is something fundamentally wrong with me, and that's why all this has happened. I will say that it helps to be clear about what is actually happening in my head.

———— ∞ ————

Joy discovered an important truth as she was going through the summer of her grief. There is a recurring theme that seems to come up at the most unpredictable times, and it's the double-barrel shotgun of guilt and shame. Guilt is focused on things that we could have legitimately done but just didn't for whatever reason. Guilt focuses entirely on our decisions and behaviors that clearly in the future we can correct when we get the chance.

On the other hand, shame is focused entirely on our person or our being. It's because of who we are that all the bad things happened to us. If we were just better people or different somehow, then what happened wouldn't have happened. The worse part of shame and these attacks is that they tempt us into comparing our journey through grief with other people's journeys. Everyone else's journey looks better, smoother, and easier. But ours seems to be particularly difficult. The only reasonable conclusion is that the difference lies in the nature of who we are, not the decisions we have made, and if we could have changed ourselves, then none of this would have happened to us.

The key thing to understand is that shame focuses on the outcome and judges our worth as a person because of it. Changing our person is by no means an easy thing to do, and therefore, we are pretty much doomed to live the rest of our lives this way.

Joy chose a very effective tool to use during the summer of her grief, which was to take the time to reflect and journal about what was happening. We cannot fight an enemy that we have not named. She did an effective job of naming what her adversary was—shame or guilt—and would make the appropriate adjustments to prevent it from happening in the future. When she identified that it was shame that was operational, then her strategies had to change entirely. That is the challenge in the summer of our grief. It seems that using our journals is pretty easy because our shredded hearts are a "target-rich" environment. There are emotions leaking out everywhere. But as we get more acclimated to the journey through our grief, we tend to take for granted the progress we are making, and we forget that the tools that were so helpful then can be just as helpful now.

25

FORGIVENESS?

"Forgiveness is the name of love practiced among people who love poorly."
—Henri Nouwen

"You know, after all this time that we have spent processing your grief and walking this journey through your grief, I haven't heard you say anything about Caleb." Tricia started out the counseling with a bang.

Joy was not expecting such a blunt question right away. Over the course of the last months, she and Tricia would always do a little warm-up talking about the week's events since the last counseling session and other minor details of her life. It seemed to ease the wading into the shockingly cold water of her emotions and thoughts. Joy was caught off guard and looked at Tricia blankly.

"Don't get me wrong, Joy, I'm not assuming that you 'should' be talking about Caleb by now, but with all the walking you've done through some pretty intense anger, I would have thought Caleb would be one of the top vote-getters for your anger and sadness over being taken advantage of like you were." Tricia was knowingly or unknowingly buying Joy some time to collect her thoughts, which was a relief. Tricia's question had made Joy feel like someone had splashed her with a bucket of ice water.

"Actually, you're right, Trish. I've been avoiding that topic because I simply don't know where to go with it all.

Caleb is long gone, and my ability to have any access to him is equally gone. I have rehearsed in my head many times what I would say to him, but I always end up at the same place asking myself, *Why invest all that energy when you'll never get the chance to confront him about happened and the heartache I have gone through as a result?*"

"There's another side of that coin, too, that I struggle with," she continued. "Which is that it was me who chose to go along with all his pressuring about sex. I should have just said no, and it would have never happened." Her voice trailed off as she thought back on that night, and felt the "if onlys" moving back into her head.

"Okay, I'll get back to Caleb in a sec," Trish said. "But I want you to tap the brakes a bit before you keep rolling down that road of shame and the 'what ifs' that haunt so many people who look back on their decisions and experience the kind of regret you're at least hinting at. You're engaging in what everyone would identify as twenty-twenty hindsight and then holding yourself accountable for what you should have known but didn't. I realize that knowledge is very different from experience, particularly in this department, but at the same time it's important to validate what we feel *right now* while looking clear-eyed at the past without distorting it."

Joy nodded, but she was already feeling swept up in the narratives that run so loudly in her head about what she could have done differently.

Trish noticed Joy's distractedness and interrupted with, "Where's your head right now, Joy?"

"I feel like I've gotten swept along in the wave of all that regret and all the 'should haves.' I'm not sure how to get out of it." Joy looked at her with a pleading look in her eyes, and Trish responded quickly.

"Okay, Joy, let's switch gears and get back to Caleb, shall we?" she said steadily.

"Okay, what about Caleb?" Joy responded. She felt that she was turning the corner and could see some emotional daylight with this shift of focus.

"So, where are you with him at this point?" Trish asked.

"It's like I said before, since I don't have any access to him, it feels like a dead end in terms of what I do with my feelings toward him." Joy was breathing a little more easily now.

"What if I told you that there is a way to cut him loose and finally be free of him once and for all? Would you be interested?"

"Sure, but what could that be, Trish? I alternate between blaming him and being really angry and hurt about what happened, and then blaming myself and being angry with and punishing myself."

"What about forgiving him, Joy?" Trish paused to see what her reaction would be.

"Forgiving him! You're out of your mind, Trish! It would be like this catastrophe never happened. And everything he did to leave us stranded and me alone to face my little boy dying was cruel, and I just give him a pass? No way, no way! Hell no! I ain't doing it!" Joy's blood was boiling, and she could barely contain herself at the thought of Caleb getting off the hook like that. She strongly considered getting up and walking out.

"There's the anger I was suspecting was there all along." Trish wasn't being smug at all; instead, she was clearly and genuinely accepting of all the anger that Joy had been holding back for so long. "I figured that, that intensity of anger was there, but it's that intensity that scares us all because we fear that it predicts us becoming an angry person. Which isn't true, just a profoundly hurt person, that's all." Trish's voice was empathetic and comforting, even though Joy was still shaking from the anger and rage she was feeling.

"So, let me explain, okay?" She looked at Joy to make sure she was willing to listen.

"Forgiveness is a separate process altogether from repentance and reconciliation. You don't have to have Caleb confess and repent in order for you to forgive him. How you handle your forgiveness is between you and God. My shorthand way of thinking about forgiveness is 'releasing the other person from my demand that he change.' Forgiveness cancels the debt the other person owes us for the wrong he or she has done to us. Is that fair? Of course not! Does that change them? Maybe. The change that someone else needs to make is between them and God. Does that impact other people? Yes! Of course it does! But when we are hurt, the thing we have to work through is our forgiveness of the other person. It's important to understand that forgiveness is not only a decision, but there is also a process of releasing that is part of forgiveness." As Joy listened, Trish explained the landscape of forgiveness and how important it is to healing our grief.

What Trish explained in this conversation is particularly true when someone had some responsibility or role to play in the death of our loved one. The fascinating thing about forgiveness is that the process of forgiveness is a lot like the process of healing from our grief. There is denial or minimizing at first, and then there is anger that is turned outward toward whoever was involved, whether they had responsibility or not. The next stage is when our anger turns inward on us and all that we could have done or should have done to prevent the loss from happening. Those are natural phases of the grieving process, and they are integral to the various seasons of our grief as well. The reality is that these stages show up in all of the grief seasons in one form or another. When we choose to release someone from our demand for punishment or our unwillingness to forgive them, we are actually freeing ourselves more so than the other person. The thing to keep in mind is that our demands on the other person keep us chained to that person, and I'm convinced that we would rather not be tied to someone who may have had a hand in our loss and subsequent grief we experienced. Our grief is the same way—with winter (denial), spring (the reawakening of emotions including anger), summer (adjusting to our new environment), and fall (the re-emergence of "color" to our lives and our reinvestment in relationships while holding a place in our heart for the person who has left us behind). The process of forgiveness is embedded in the journey of our grief. There are successive opportunities or invitations to release the person who has left us, and in so doing we will be releasing ourselves to further heal from the pain of our loss.

26

A SPIRITUAL CRISIS

"Crisis is what suppressed pain looks like; it always comes to the surface. It shakes you into reflection and healing."
—Bryant McGill

A few days after Joy's session with her counselor, Meg stopped by as she was walking and asked Joy if she wanted to join her. Joy was very ready to debrief after that counseling session. There were still things about what Trish said that were really bugging her, and she was having a hard time identifying them.

"So, how's it going, Joy?" Meg started out as they were underway.

"I don't know actually. I had a counseling session a few days ago, and we talked about the idea of forgiving Caleb for doing what he did and all the pain I went through as a result. I realized that I was way more angry than I had paid attention to, but even as I was walking away, I realized that I was really angry at God too. I have pretty much walked away from the church because I got tired of the spiritual platitudes that people were throwing at me without really knowing much of my story. Church just wasn't much of a safe place anymore, and God was even less safe because of what happened with Aaron." Joy had opened the floodgates of her thoughts and emotions, and it was pretty hard to hold it all back.

"Well, for what it's worth, I'm thankful you took me up on my offer. For some reason, I had a prompting in my heart that I needed to check in with you. Even if you do hate God, I believe He prompted me to invite you." Meg smiled.

"Yeah, I'm not real sure what to do with that, but I'm glad you asked. I really needed some time to debrief what I have been wrestling with the last few days." Joy shrugged her shoulders and took a sip of her coffee that she had brought with her.

"So, tell me, Joy, what's the anger at God all about?" Meg looked over with compassion.

"Well, I guess there are a couple of things. First, if God is so good and so powerful, why didn't He save Aaron, like prompting me to notice sooner what was going on so I could've gotten help earlier? The second thing is that if God's people are supposed to be the safest community available to us, why is it that so many people I meet seem incapable of just affirming the pain I'm in and letting that be enough? I thought they were supposed to be following Jesus. What still sticks in my head from a podcast I listened to is Jesus's reaction when his friend Lazarus died and Lazarus's sisters were angry at Him. He didn't spout a platitude or say, 'Everything is going to be better, just give it time.' He was able to hear them out and not jump on them for not trusting Him."

Meg was listening intently, then paused before she replied, "Listen, Joy, I'm not going to blast you with ill-timed truth instead of affirming your hurt and pain. That's where platitudes come in, used often to try to ease the sense of helplessness the other person feels rather than what the grieving person needs. I will say this. I think we have to sort out what perspective we are viewing God from rather than assuming that our perspective is always right. When I look at God through the lens of my pain and sorrow, He often seems distant, aloof, and uncaring because that's what we feel . . . very alone. On the other hand, if when I'm ready I can remind myself of God's heart for me and my sorrow and pain, then such demands to ease that pain become less insistent. You used a great example from the death of Lazarus. When Jesus arrived, Martha and Mary both had the same response to Him, a little like you're having. 'Where were you when we needed you?' We're actually told, if you read it carefully, that Martha goes charging out to Jesus and really gets in His face about it. They both had faith that Jesus knew what He was doing and He would be faithful as he had always been, but the confusion and pain were blinding both of them. In other words, you're not alone, and you're actually in pretty good company."

"I guess I never thought of it that way. It's pretty easy to fall into the trap of looking for someone to blame, and God is a pretty easy one to point the finger at since He is all-powerful and good."

"Hold on a sec with that about Him being good," Meg interrupted. "I think we have to be really careful about defining good in terms of what we determine is good, and as long as God complies with that, then He is 'good.' I understand that feeling completely, since I have struggled with this too. But just remember that as long as God is good according to our definitions, then we really don't have to trust Him to know better than we do. We actually see lots of examples of this kind of struggle in Job's story. So sorry I interrupted you." Meg looked back at her.

"No worries, I appreciate you clarifying that for me. I'm still mad at Him, God I mean, and I've still got to struggle through this, but I needed to hear someone else's perspective about it who's been through this before," Joy replied.

"Now, about the people in the church. I will agree with you that, that is the most irritating thing to face about church. You're not wrong that church is supposed to be safe for suffering and grieving people, but unfortunately, the rest of the congregation, wherever that is for you, hasn't gotten the message yet. Taking a break from church probably isn't such a bad idea, Joy. I stayed away for quite a while, not because I was condemning them for being that way, but because I wasn't willing to risk getting hit with that kind of stuff. It was hard enough during the week, I didn't need to get hit with it on Saturday or Sunday too." Joy nodded in agreement as she was talking.

"That's a relief to hear you say that, Meg. I was beginning to think that I was committing some mortal sin by not going. I may go back eventually, but I just can't take it right now. It's one thing to fight this battle and this journey through my grief; it's quite another to have to battle that too."

———

During the summer of our grief, we will often face a spiritual crisis much like Joy is experiencing. All of her assumptions and notions about God were getting blown up, and she confronted a choice to make. Either leave her faith entirely, including the church, or seek someone who has walked this journey before and understands the landscape so they can help us process our thoughts and feelings. We don't need someone to throw more Bible verses at us, because we are already doubting God's goodness and faithfulness, so hearing from Scripture isn't much help. We need someone who will give us the space to voice our anger, our concerns, and our other feelings before ever attempting to challenge the thoughts we have that we often label as beliefs; those thoughts are actually feelings that need to be voiced and affirmed before we ever have the ability to evaluate them. You also have to be gentle and kind with yourself in this department and not fall into the trap that you "should" be over this by now. I have presented seasons for a reason. Our grief journey is a series of cycles through each season, and different challenges await us in each season, which are all part of our healing.

27

LIKE RIDING A BIKE?

"I always did something I was a little not ready to do. I think that's how you grow. When there's that moment of 'Wow, I'm not really sure I can do this,' and you push through those moments, that's when you have a breakthrough."

—Marissa Mayer

Joy was deep in the bowels of the library in the "Rare Books" section. Sometimes she felt that it was like a black hole in the library—people go in and never come out! As she was busy putting away a few books people had checked out, she muttered under her breath, "Who reads this stuff? Wow! It looks good enough to be a great sleep medication, but what do I know!" Just as she had gotten a book situated and was moving to the next aisle over, she heard someone loudly whisper her name.

"Joy! Joy, where are you?" Joy couldn't identify the voice because whoever it was, was whispering. Joy went to the head of the aisle and looked back and forth to see who it might be. Just at that moment, Lauren popped out of another aisle a couple of rows down from her.

"Lauren! Here I am! What brings you into the morgue, aka the library, today?" Joy smiled because of just how descriptive that was for her library.

Lauren rolled her eyes and walked to her. "Joy . . . there you are! Someone up front said I might find you in the Rare Books section, so I've been wandering around for fifteen minutes trying to find where that was! It's kind of creepy down here. Do you come down here much?"

"Heavens no! I avoid it as much as I can. I fear that if I stay down here too long, I'll never come out!" Joy was quietly laughing. "What's up, Lauren? What brings you down here today?"

"Hang on a sec," Lauren said as she started rummaging through her sling pack. She finally found what she was looking for, and pulled a piece of paper out and handed it to Joy.

"What's this?" Joy scanned the piece of paper and noticed in big bold letters at the top the words "Volunteers Needed."

Lauren pulled her over to a table so they could sit. "I just saw this at my work since our organization collaborates with this shelter for single moms. The more I read the qualifications for who they're looking for, the more I thought of you as a perfect fit." Lauren looked at her hopefully with a smile on her face.

"Interesting . . ." Joy continued to read the qualifications in the flyer. The shelter was looking for young women desiring to come alongside and befriend young new single moms, helping them to get employed and to learn how to balance the demands of single parenthood.

"I don't know, Lauren. I've been so far out of commission when it comes to relationships like this, I'm not sure I could do it." Joy looked up at Lauren.

"Oh, come on, Joy! You'd be great at it. You have a kind heart, you're a great listener, and it might actually do you good to help another young woman who is in the same place as you would have been not all that long ago. Just because your little boy died doesn't make you any less of a mom."

The next day, Joy had the day off, so she drove over to the shelter for single moms she'd read about in the flyer Lauren had given her. She thought she would check it out and see how she might fit in. If it was a good fit, she would be using old skills that she had a while ago before Aaron was born. She had previously volunteered as a paraprofessional in the school system, and during that time she met with plenty of single moms picking their kids up, and of course, she always found herself absolutely adoring the kids.

When she arrived, she walked up the front steps to the Victorian house that looked anything but a shelter for single moms. It was very comfortable and inviting to anyone walking down the street. As she walked in, a bell rang indicating that someone was coming through the front door. Shortly, a tall young woman came out into the foyer smiling broadly.

"Hi! My name is Amanda and I'm the house coordinator here at Hope House. What can I do for you?"

"Hi, Amanda. I'm Joy, and a friend of mine gave me a flyer that you were looking for volunteers to help with the young women here?"

"Oh yes! That's wonderful, Joy! We are a nonprofit organization that provides a safe place for young moms and their kids. They may have been kicked out of their homes for getting pregnant or had their own fair share of shame and couldn't face anyone. What matters is that they come to us for shelter, training, and job referrals to get them back on their feet. The type of volunteer we are looking for is someone who can be a mentor for one of these young ladies and just meet with her every week or so and be there for the ins and outs of life with a baby. It's not a huge demand on your time, but it is incredibly valuable to them to have someone who will be in their corner as they struggle to get independent again." Amanda looked at her hopefully as if she was waiting for her to bolt out the door.

"I'm in!" said Joy. What Amanda didn't know was what was building inside Joy that felt like a well of compassion and an intense desire to help in whatever way she could. She didn't even factor in where she was in her own grief journey. The desire to help was so strong that Joy felt like her heart was beating faster the more Amanda described what she was doing.

"Wow! Great! I'll tell you what, let me show you around, and then we can find a time for our prospective mentors to do a meet-and-greet with those of our residents who need a mentor." Amanda was having a hard time hiding her enthusiasm as she spoke.

———⊗⊗⊗———

What you have portrayed here is the next steps into the summer of Joy's grief. This season involves trying on new roles or dusting off old skills to be applied in new settings. There is a certain amount of lethargy to grief that is often shaken up during the summer. We want to start spreading our wings, but at times we are held back because it feels like we are leaving the person we have lost behind. We also struggle with figuring out whether it's the time to start pushing that envelope. Up until this time we have been encouraged to "be gentle" and to "be kind" to ourselves during this process, but it is during this season that we begin to feel the urge to spread our wings and try something new. That's great, but just remember that not everything we try turns out to be a perfect fit, and that's okay. It's a process of trying something and, if it doesn't work, then turning our attention to trying something else, whether that's a skill or even a different role than the one with which we have grown familiar. That's where the kindness comes in. Allow attempts like these to fail without falling into the trap of thinking nothing will work. Actually it's kindness with ourselves and our halting attempts to try new things *and* patience if it doesn't work right away. We don't recover from our grief overnight; it will take trial and error to get through this leg of the journey.

28

A New Kind of Shock

"You've got to be kidding me, Dad! You have a girl-friend?" Ben was beside himself when his dad told him that he was dating someone. It had been about ten months since his mom died, and to him it seemed way too soon for his dad to start up another relationship with a woman.

Ben had come home to visit. That summer he had an internship in the same city where his university was, so he took a long weekend to go visit his dad and sister. As he was driving home, he was mulling over all the things that had changed for him since he had last been home. Working with family members of cancer patients was certainly the highlight of this past year. He had graduated college this year, so the last time he had seen his dad and sister was at graduation. It was a very bittersweet moment where Ben bounced between profoundly missing his mom and wishing she was there for all the festivities and just enjoying all the work that had gone into these last four years of school.

He had gotten home in the late afternoon, and his dad wasn't home, which he thought was a little odd but didn't give it much thought. Later that evening his dad came rolling in at nine thirty. Ben had already been home for six hours.

He had had time to wash his clothes and take a nap. He had even prepared his own dinner and eaten it alone. It felt a little like the days during his internship but at his family's home rather than his apartment. Something was really wrong, but he didn't know what that might be.

He was in the living room playing on his Nintendo Switch when his dad came in the front door. "Hey, Ben! I'm home! So sorry, I had intended on being home sooner, but it just didn't quite work out that way." Ben's dad was turning around from throwing his shoes in the hall closet when Ben came in from the living room.

"Wow! Have roles changed now or what?" Ben said with thick sarcasm in his voice. He had a smirk on his face as his dad looked up.

"Huh? What do you mean?" his dad replied. He was being a little evasive for Ben's liking. It was downright shocking to see his dad acting this way.

"I hate to sound like you when I was in high school, but where were you? I got home six, count them six, hours ago! What's going on?" Ben was working hard to veil his suspicion and anger about what he suspected was going on.

"Okay, okay, sorry. I don't mean to be so evasive. I've been meaning to tell you when we talk on the phone, but I just couldn't bring myself to say it. I feared that it would really upset you going into finals . . ." His dad's voice trailed off.

"Wait! What? You mean that your relationship with whoever you are seeing started back up when I was in finals?" Ben's internal temperature was rising, and he could feel his heart beating faster. "Okay, enough. Just spill it, will ya, Dad?"

His dad took a deep breath and looked him in the eye. "Yes, I am seeing another woman. Her name is Joan. She was a new hire at work who came from another engineering firm. I was put in charge of helping her get onboarded to our company. The more we talked, the more we realized we had in common. We both have kids grown and out of the house, or almost, and a spouse who died. Both of us love traveling, and we're both pretty good engineers." His dad beamed brightly as he thought about his new girlfriend.

"Wow, Dad! I'll admit, it's pretty hard for me to get overly excited about it all, but I can say that I don't understand what it's like to lose a spouse. But, Dad, isn't it too soon? We're only ten months away from Mom dying!"

"What's too soon or too long, Ben?" his dad shot back.

"I don't know. It just feels too soon to start up another relationship with a woman when Mom's memory is still so fresh."

His dad was nodding. "Yeah, yeah, I get that. I guess when I started feeling this way, it actually took me by surprise. I wasn't looking for a relationship at all. But I will say it is so comforting to have a woman in my life again. No one really told me when the 'right time' would be."

Ben had his face in his hands. "Oh geez, Dad, really? You've got to be kidding me!"

———— ∞ ————

As we move into the fall of our grief, many more colors seem to be clear and even exciting to see. This includes new relationships. Taking the risk of losing someone again is quite a mountain to climb, yet it may be that something is telling us we are ready when we experience what Ben's dad did when similar feelings or love and attraction being emerging for a new person. This season is not marked by forgetting the person we have lost but by keeping a place for him or her in our memories as we begin to invest back into life again. Up to this point, we have been confronted with grieving tasks, at first hot and heavy and then more steadily as the journey has continued. In a metaphorical sense, we haven't felt that we had the time to stop and smell or even look at the roses. In this season, we are entering a new vista of our journey where it seems to come alive with the colors of relationships, opportunities for growth, and further investment in the future. All the work up to this point has been building to this season. The tasks are not over, and the tools we've used are still going to be needed, but we won't have to lean on them as much as we once did.

Ben is feeling the sting of his dad moving into this season ahead of him. The reality is that the resistance Ben is voicing is the voice of comfort with the known features of the journey he has gotten accustomed to up to this point. Changing those up can sometimes feel like another loss, just a different kind. It's the loss of growth and change. There are always going to be points like this when we will have to make the choice to be uncomfortable in the name of growth. It's far from easy, and it often come in fits and starts.

We don't think anything about it when we see little kids grow up and they have growth spurts; what we don't notice is that such spurts in growth always come with some changes or challenges for the child. Why should we be any different in our growth and healing through grief? Just because we are adults doesn't make us immune to such regressions and progressions. When it comes to our journey through the seasons of grief, just like in seasons in nature, we will have challenges in each season. While these challenges indicate that we are growing and, because of this, are welcome, the challenges still remain difficult and uncomfortable. These challenges indicate that we are not losing ground but growing.

29

Feeling Better but Guilty

"When a loved one passes, there are mixed emotions,
and a thirst to live one's own life more deeply can
certainly be among them."

—Salli Richardson

The weekend passed without much fanfare. Ben got a chance to meet Joan over dinner, and he was pleasantly surprised to see his dad so animated and engaging with this new woman in his life. He seemed to exude vitality that had been missing for so long. Ben walked away smiling and gratified that his dad was doing so well and feeling so much better. There had been some pretty dark days during the early months after his mom had died. His dad had seemed lost and very shaken. But not tonight. He was laughing and having fun with Joan, and it did Ben good to see his dad so happy. Even in that, he felt a little guilty and disloyal to his mom for directing his loyalty to someone else. He wasn't real sure what to make of it, so he called up his friend Greg and scheduled to have coffee together later in the week.

Both Ben and Greg arrived at the same time, so they walked in and ordered their coffee and wandered over to find a table within earshot of their drinks being called.

Greg started by saying, "So, what's this all about, Ben? I hadn't heard from you in a while. I figured you were busy with your internship, but when you called and were a little vague about the subject, I must say my curiosity was piqued."

"Greg, cafe latte, and Ben, a cappuccino!" the barista called out.

"Hang on a sec, I'll get them." Greg gestured for Ben to stay seated.

Greg returned and slid Ben's cappuccino over to him. "Thanks," Ben replied. "Yeah, I realize I was a little evasive on the phone, but I wasn't in a place to talk freely in my office. Otherwise, I would have given you a better heads-up. Sorry about that."

"Don't sweat it," Greg said, waving it off.

He picked up where they left off. "So what's up?"

"Well, news from the home front. My dad has a girl-friend!" Ben paused for effect.

Greg's eyebrows raised, and he whispered, "What?"

"Yep, he hit me with the news last weekend, and I got to meet her a couple of days later. Now, don't get me wrong, She seems to be a really nice person. What's even more remarkable is seeing my dad that happy. He hasn't been that happy in a long, long time. So that's good, I guess." Ben's tone of voice was a bit tentative.

"Okay, okay, I get that, but what's bothering you about it? After all, that sounds like a truly positive development for your dad and your family." Greg smiled broadly.

"Yeah, I guess so. I guess what bothers me is that there is some shine taken off my delight for my dad. As a matter of fact, I feel this tinge of guilt as I was getting to know Joan—that's her name—and even feeling positive about her. I mean, there was really nothing to dislike, but even feeling positive felt a little weird."

"Okay, Ben, so tell me. What was your first reaction when your dad told you about Joan?" Greg asked.

"Oh man, I was furious and hurt all at the same time. Like he had betrayed Christine and me by going off with another woman. Now that I think of it, I probably felt jealous too," Ben replied.

Greg nodded, "So what was it you were so furious and jealous about?"

Ben didn't know why his jealousy was such a big deal to Greg. There was nothing to react to from Ben's perspective. Since the weekend had turned out pretty well, that was enough. But he played along. "I guess my flash of anger and jealousy was because he was moving on from Mom . . . and us."

Greg was nodding even more vigorously. "Like you didn't expect this to happen so soon, and you really hadn't thought through the fact that your dad would pursue life away from your mom, right?"

"Yeah, exactly. I said it was too soon, but the more I thought about it, I realized I would never want to stand in the way of my dad being happy. I guess my sense of loyalty is still pretty strong to my mom. It kinda felt like my dad had announced he was having an affair." Ben shrugged because he knew the moment it came out of his mouth that it was unfair and didn't really make much sense.

"Okay, so let me see if I've got this straight. You felt that your dad was being disloyal to your mom and her memory?" Greg asked.

"Yep, pretty much. I think that's where the jealousy was coming from. I was jealous for my mom even though she's gone." Ben looked down suddenly when he had to admit once again that his mom was out of their lives.

"What about you and your loyalty to your mom?" Greg asked.

"What do you mean, my loyalty?" Ben was confused.

"So you said that the rest of the weekend went pretty well, and you were happy to see your dad so happy, but you ended up walking away feeling a little guilty, right?"

"Yep." Ben wasn't sure where Greg was going with this, but now he was curious.

"Could it be, Ben, that you were feeling positive and encouraged about Joan, and that triggered a challenge to your own loyalty to your mom? It would signal that you were taking a step away from your mom, and you're not so sure that you're quite ready for that. Your dad might be, but you're not." Greg paused to let it all sink in for Ben, so he took a gulp of his latte.

"I guess I never thought about my loyalty to my mom. I knew it was there, but just not that strong," Ben said thoughtfully.

"Your dad managed to unearth it when he himself took a step away from your mom. I'm not sure you know how your dad got to that point, but it would sure be worth finding out. Everybody takes the journey of grief at a different pace. You and your dad are really no different."

———— ∞ ————

During the fall season of our grief, while the color seems to have returned to our world and exciting new relationships and possibilities seem to be before us, it is almost inevitable, though not predictable, that we will feel a tinge of guilt for moving on when our lost one can't move on with us. That is truly a pothole of sorts on the road of grief. By the time we get to this place in our journey through grief, we don't anticipate the cost of leaving the people we care deeply about behind. That doesn't mean that we have to forget them, but part of the task of moving through this season is finding a way to carve out a space in our hearts for our loved one to inhabit or exist in without cutting ourselves off from them. It can be a treasured memento from them, or a favorite story or poet that we shared with them that we can return to and read and remember them. I have one of those mementos for my dad who died when I was twelve. It is hanging around my neck and probably will do so until the end of my days. It is a reminder of him and his influence on me.

Interestingly, God knew that we needed to have specific objects and actions to remember important things about Him as well. Probably one of the most important sacraments in the church is the Last Supper, and when Jesus instituted it for the first time, He said, "Do this as you remember me." So, items like a cross or a tattoo that we wear to permanently remind of us of His love and grace are all examples of that. The power of these tokens or keepsakes from the people who have died in our lives serve as an external or physical reminder of the space they inhabit in our hearts. Feeling better is not a signal that we are forgetting, but an indication of our willingness to journey into the future without them.

30

A NECESSARY GOOD-BYE

*"Farewell has a sweet sound of reluctance. Good-bye is
short and final, a word with teeth sharp to bite through
the string that ties past to the future."*
—John Steinbeck

After Greg and Ben's conversation at the coffee house, Ben decided that he would make an appointment with the counselor he had been talking to just as he was trying to recover from his grief. He was very helpful then, and Ben wondered if he would be helpful now that it appeared as if he was beginning to feel better. So, he called and set up a time for them to meet.

Dr. Wheatley came to the waiting room door and waved at Ben to follow him back to his office. He no sooner got the door closed before he greeted Ben, saying, "Hey, Ben! Good to see you again. How's it going?"

Ben got situated in his favorite chair in Dr. Wheatley's office, and Dr. Wheatley situated himself in the chair across from him. "It's been going well, Dr. Wheatley. You'll be happy to hear that my dad has begun to get involved in another relationship. Her name is Joan, and I haven't seen him this happy in quite some time." Ben was smiling as he made his report to the psychologist.

"I'm thrilled to hear that about your dad, Ben! So, what about you? How's the journey going, and how's your heart these days?" Ever the counselor, Dr. Wheatley redirected their conversation to Ben.

"I think I'm doing pretty well. I'm still going to the grief group you recommended off and on as time allows. It's been good, and I think I'm coming out into some breathing space with my grief. It just seems like my world has more colors in it than it had before, and some are pretty bright."

"That's good to hear, Ben! That's a long way from the young man who came in and indicated that he was only here to please his dad!" Dr. Wheatley smiled.

"So, while I'm delighted to see you again, Ben, why are you coming in now just when things seem to be going so well?" He looked at Ben as if he was confused.

Ben knew better. Dr. Wheatley was rarely confused; he would often bait Ben into being more specific about what his real issue was.

Ben took the bait. "Actually, it's two things, Doc. The first is my dad's new girlfriend and how I feel about her. The second is how guilty I have felt feeling anything positive about her. So, what do you think?"

"Well, let me ask you a couple of questions first, Ben. Is that okay?" Dr. Wheatley paused.

"Yeah, yeah, sure. Why is it I can't get a straight answer out of you, Doc?" Ben replied, smiling.

"Any answer, straight or otherwise, can only be built on a clear sense of context, and your description of what is going on has me feeling like I just got dropped into the middle of a movie! I'm sharp, but not that sharp, Ben!" Dr. Wheatley said, laughing at his self-deprecating humor.

Ben waved him forward, so Dr Wheatley continued. "First, how do you feel about this new girlfriend of your dad's?"

"I don't know, it's this strange mixture between feeling positive because my dad is so happy and feeling threatened because it feels like he's leaving his family." Ben thought to say more, but stopped and looked at Dr. Wheatley.

"His family? Or leaving you?" The psychologist left the question hanging out there.

"Well, I guess it's a little bit of both. I get jealous for Christine who still needs her dad during this time of her grief. She's making progress, but still struggling more than my dad and I are," Ben answered.

He thought for a second and then added, "Not only that, it feels like he has floored the accelerator to zoom way out in front of Chris and me, leaving us in the dust. I guess the answer to your question is yes and yes!"

"Okay, Ben, let me cut to the chase here and give you some food for thought at this place in your journey. It seems to me that you are at the place in your grief process to say a 'final' good-bye."

"Whoa, whoa, Doc! I thought I've already done that with this *process*, as you call it. Isn't that enough?" Ben shot back.

"Sometimes when we get to this season of our grief, which would be considered summer, we need to do something physical, you know, something like a ritual that will allow the past to influence and impact us, but we are also shifting our eyes to the future, which means jobs, relationships, and our path forward." Dr. Wheatley paused to see if Ben was following him.

Ben seemed to be struggling to wrap his head around what exactly Dr. Wheatley was trying to say. "I'll tell you what, let me describe it another way. I think you have done enough hiking in the mountains and backcountry to be familiar with cairns, right?"

Ben nodded in agreement. "Good. In a way, this final good-bye is a cairn that marks a significant point on your journey of life. Needless to say, your mom is that person. The cairn indicates physically that you will remember, and there *is* a place in your heart for her, but you are moving into the future *with that* rather than staying in the past to hang on to it. Does that help any?" Dr. Wheatley looked over at Ben.

"Yeah, it does. Is there any form to this saying good-bye?" Ben asked.

Dr. Wheatley nodded, "Yeah, but to some degree each person has to figure out what most embodied his or her relationship with that person. Sometimes people will write a letter that they read at the grave, or they just go to the grave and start talking and let the tears and thoughts flow until there is nothing more to say. Others will do some combination of those things, but I've seen people do all kinds of rituals like this. Sometimes they involve other people, sometimes they do it alone. That's entirely up to them."

"Okay, Dr. Wheatley. I think it get it. I'll mull it over and if I have any questions, do you mind if I email you or something?" Ben's mind was already forming a plan that would help him do something like what Dr. Wheatley was suggesting.

When we arrive at the fall of our grief, we can finally emotionally breathe, and like Ben, it seems like color has returned to our world that up until now has been whites, grays, and blacks. Dr. Wheatley points out, quite accurately, that Ben sounded like he needed a ritual to mark coming to the end of his journey. It's important to remember, though, that just because we might do something like this, it doesn't mean that everything is smooth sailing from here on out. Far from it. Life changes, we change, relationships come and go, and as discouraging as it might be to hear, losses don't just stop either. Don't forget, though, that there are strategies and perspectives that you have gained during this journey that can be applied over and over again.

31

LETTERS TO THE FUTURE

"You can't go back and change the beginning, but you can start where you are and change the ending."
—C.S. Lewis

This was probably the most difficult drive Ben had ever taken. It felt a little like a private odyssey not only in search of himself but to get a glimpse of the future. He began to understand the desire for more that drove pioneers, treasure hunters, and the people who seemed to push the boundaries of imagination through what they wrote. There is always a quest, the trials faced during that quest, and if the hero or heroine is up to the task, achieving the prize. In Ben's case, it wasn't a prize; it was a grave that was awaiting him. He hadn't been there for at least ten months, and so much had happened during that time. He had graduated with a business degree and gotten involved in a couple of different ministries, all the while doing the grief work that Dr. Wheatley and the guys in his grief group encouraged him to do. His dad had started a new relationship, and Ben was warming up to the new woman in his dad's life, albeit at a glacial pace.

He pulled into the cemetery, and it felt like he was hyperventilating. He couldn't breathe, and suddenly it felt like the past and the present were merged. The sights, sounds, and even smells of that funeral day were vividly bombarding him. At the same time, the cemetery was pretty empty, and finding his way to his mom's grave gave his memory a bit of a stretch looking for the landmarks that would indicate he was in the right sector of the cemetery where his mom was buried.

Then he saw it. The headstone was unique because his dad didn't want the usual polished marble rectangle for their headstone. He wanted something that would convey something of Ben's mom's personality. It was a rough-hewn stone that looked like it had just come from the stone quarry. She hated what she thought was the obsession to look the "right" way. She always wanted to be a person who was in the process of growth which at times would not look all "buttoned up" all the time. She was a non-conformist at heart not to make a point but to reflect the reality of her own soul. The upright stone sat on an equally rough-hewn base and had their family name and underneath the names Gwen Ruth and Robert William engraved. When Ben looked at the stone, he caught his breath. It was like seeing these names literally written in stone had stabbed him in the heart with the reality he had been wrestling with. Kind of like when your enemy who has been shrouded in smoke and clouds is suddenly revealed for the first time.

There was a grassy spot in front of the gravestone, so Ben sat down and pulled out his note for his mom. He read it aloud as he sat facing the headstone.

Dear Mom,

I don't really know how to start this, but I think I'm going to focus on what happened after you died, and then where I am now, and then where I'm going from here.

Wow! So much has changed since you left, or should I say were taken. Your absence threw our family into total chaos, which only says how much you held us all together. I can't tell you how much I miss you, Mom.

Ben paused as the emotions welled up and felt like they were going to choke him. The tears flowed freely, and it took him a while to compose himself enough to continue reading. He couldn't see the paper. Finally, the flow of tears slowed and he was able to breathe again. He took a deep breath and kept going.

Something I have learned during this time since you've been away is that tears are an indication of our love for the person we've lost. There is no reason to apologize for them. I'm beginning to understand just how much I loved you. I knew that then, but I just didn't communicate that to you enough, and for that I have a lot of regret. I will certainly be more purposeful from now on communicating to the people I love how much I love them, leaving no doubt.

But I'm getting ahead of myself. I miss talking to you each weekend like I did while I was in school. You always said just what I needed to hear . . . sometimes I liked it and other times I didn't. And even if I didn't, you didn't back down, but instead allowed me the freedom to accept or reject it. I now realize how incredibly unique that was. Of course you're my mom; you're going to legitimately get frustrated with my stubbornness and shortsightedness.

Dad really struggled with your absence. He seemed like a lost puppy the first few months. It took him months to get rid of your favorite chair that was in your bedroom. He didn't donate your clothes to other people who might need them(which you would have done) because they had your perfume on them, and it meant a little more of you was going away.

Christine has struggled a lot with your absence. She was just so angry at first, and it was all that Dad and I could do to support and encourage her. She eventually came around, and got involved in a group like I did, and found a lot of help and guidance learning how to navigate life without you.

Well, that's kind of where I've been, and now here I am sitting at your graveside, remembering every-thing about that day we said good-bye and the time in between. You'll be relieved to know that I'm doing much better today. Dad is dating a new lady who is really great, and Christine and I are warming up to her. I don't think I can bring myself to say that I love her, but just the fact that Dad is so happy is enough for me to drop some of my walls.

So, where do I go from here? You will always be . . .

Ben broke into tears again. He knew what was coming in what he wrote, and it was really hard just to speak the words.

He wiped the tears away and cleared his throat to start again.

You will always be in my heart, and you've left so many memories and fingerprints on all that I do and all that I am. I would never be the man I am today without having the mom that I do, or did. It's time to do the hardest thing I've ever had to do, Mom. It's time to say good-bye. Good-bye, and I will always love you.

Ben stood and fished into his pocket and found what he was looking for. His lighter. He folded up the letter he had written, then lit it and laid it in front of the gravestone. He stood there watching it burn, and before long it turned into black wisps of ash, and before long it was gone. He was reflecting on what this all meant, but he was afraid to even leave the grave. Finally, he took a deep breath and said, "Good-bye, Mom." He turned and walked to his car and drove home.

⁂

Sometimes it is important to engage in rituals like this. We have very little in our worlds that marks time for us. Somehow rituals have come to feel like an interruption to our overcommitment to happiness and good times. Unfortunately, with our commitment to forget about the past and all that was bad there, we have also thrown out the things that were important to connect us powerfully to the past. That's what rituals do for us. Take the time to remember the past in order to move forward into the future with clarity, purpose, and freedom.

32

FOREST OR TREES?

"In a forest of a hundred thousand trees, no two leaves are alike.
And no two journeys along the same path are alike."
—Paulo Coelho

Ben was just finishing up his first full month at his new job. He had accepted a position at an up-and-coming social media firm. His internship had prepared him well for the variety of tasks he was facing and was responsible for now that he was getting paid for what he was doing. It was weird not starting another school year. He had gotten accustomed to the structure and predictability of school, and now there wasn't that structure. Just work to be done and projects to complete.

His phone buzzed just as he was packing up to go home.

"Hello?" Ben answered as he slung his messenger bag over his shoulder.

"Hey, Ben! How ya doing? Nate here. How's the new job treating you?" Nate said with a lot more enthusiasm than he himself had.

"Hi, Nate! It's going well," Ben replied. He set his bag down and moved over to his desk. "What can I do for you?"

"I haven't seen you in a while at group other than, when was that, a couple of months ago?"

"Yeah, that sounds about right. Hey listen, I'm just walking out the door. How about I call you when I get home, and we can catch up a bit?" Ben asked.

"Sure, that's fine," Nate responded. "I've just got an idea that I wanted to run past you and see what you thought."

"Okay, that'll be great. How about I call you in an hour?" Ben suggested.

"Perfect, thanks! Catch ya later!" The line went dead as Nate clicked off.

About an hour later, Ben called Nate to found out what kind of idea Nate had for him. They began the call with mostly chitchat.

"Ben, I've been thinking about something, and it's only been confirmed over the last ten minutes or so of our conversation today on the phone. As you know, at group we often have a speaker come and talk to the guys about the grieving process for men . . ."

Ben had a sinking feeling in his stomach, and a sudden rush of thoughts. I can't speak to them about grieving, what do I know? Who am I to be the "expert" about grief. I fought it half the time I was going through it. Nate has finally, completely lost his mind. He must really be hard up for someone to speak! Ben tuned back into what Nate was saying.

"Look, Ben, when I think about someone who has been through the seasons of grief, you have walked that journey in the most authentic and real way I've really ever seen. You didn't hold back or pull any punches about how tough life was and how you were doing. Both good and bad. Quite honestly, in spite of your misgivings which I know are starting to crop up in your head, I don't want the guys to get the impression that going through grief is a 'bloodless' journey. There is a cost to be paid, and it isn't easy. You're the first person I thought of to communicate that to them. More importantly, all I want for you to do is reflect for them on what your journey has been like and that's it. You don't have to teach or wrap it all up nicely in a bow. You just have to be yourself. A lot of these guys know you, and you can give them a bird's-eye view. What do you think?" Nate paused to see how Ben might respond.

Ben took a deep breath. "So let me ask you this, Nate. You're not looking for me to be the expert, right?"

"Right," Nate replied.

"You're only asking me to give them some observations about how my journey has been, right?

"Right! Will you do it?" Nate was getting more animated in his responses.

"Yeah, okay, I'll do it—" Ben didn't even complete his sentence before Nate jumped in.

"Great! I am so pumped, Ben! You have no idea. This is really the first time a member of the group has taken me up on my invitation to talk to the larger group. Dude! This is going to be awesome!"

"Oh c'mon, Nate, chill out. It's not like I'm some big name in grief and grieving or anything. Geez!" Ben was working to tamp down Nate's expectations.

"Well, I just gotta say, Ben, you've made my day! Thanks so much! I'll see you at our usual time and place. Just to warn you, our group wasn't the only men's grief group around town, and the people will often come to whatever group has a speaker in it. So, it might be pretty full compared to what you have experienced. See ya, friend!" Nate hung up.

Ben was left stunned and looking at his phone as if he was hoping Nate would call back or something.

The day came much more quickly than Ben had wanted, but for good or ill, he had thrown together a few notes and was hoping for the best.

"Okay, okay! Quiet down, everybody. Let's try to get this thing started on time for a change, shall we?" Nate was shouting over the din of about fifty guys who had shown up.

"Well, I have looked forward to this for quite some time, and I want to introduce you to Ben who has been part of my group for well over a year now. He has been the most authentic guy I have seen in a while go through this thing we call the seasons of grief. Let's welcome him with a big round of applause!" Nate waved at Ben to come up and get situated with his notes, which he did.

Ben waited until the applause died down and there was some semblance of quiet.

"Okay, okay, guys! Thanks so much for such a warm welcome! I had no idea there would there be this many of you show up! Nate, you should have warned me! I would have turned you down!"

There was a smattering of laughter in response.

"Well, guys, let me make a few observations about this journey that we refer to as the seasons of grief. When I first started this journey, I came to Nate's group kicking and screaming. My dad had coerced me into coming. I was pretty sure when I came that I was checking some box and getting my dad off my back at the same time. It was going to be once and done, and then I'd figure it out on my own. But something happened that night that took me completely off guard. There were other guys, just like me, who were sharing all kinds of stories, and a lot of them were pretty ugly. Some men were defensive and guarded like I was, and some were all-in. I was so skeptical at that point that I just assumed the all-in guys were people pleasers rather than really sharing out of any personal motivation. In either case, I had never been part of a group of guys who shared the toughest part of life— losing someone they really loved—in a way that allowed them to be vulnerable with one another. It was nothing short of remarkable, and it began my journey through the seasons."

Ben continued for another half hour or so, but the one thing he wanted to be sure he drove home was that when you start the journey of grief, it is really easy to get distracted by the individual "trees" of pain, guilt, shame, and regret, and so much more. But as you keep journeying, you begin to see some daylight ahead. All is not as dark and gloomy and painful as it was in the beginning. And then you break out into a clearing and realize that you have been navigating through a forest of trees that have been changing seasons even as you have walked. By the time you arrive, they are ablaze with color inviting you back into life with a little place in your heart reserved for the one you have loved and lost.

———— ✸ ————

God knows that we need hope at the end of our stories, and He provided it when he said in Revelation 21:4 (ESV), "He will wipe away every tear from their eyes, and death shall be no more, neither shall there be mourning, nor crying, nor pain anymore." It's important as we journey through the fall of our grief to tell our stories to others who are in a different place or season of their grief. It not only provides encouragement and hope for fellow travelers, but it also allows you to "own" your story and provides the motivation to continue the journey through the seasons to come.

33

WITHDRAWALS AND DEPOSITS

*"Grief opens a place in our hearts that we never knew
could hurt so profoundly, but it also opens this same place
to a love we never imagined possible."*
—Unknown

When Joy participated in the meet-and-greet with teenage moms at the shelter, she was drawn to one girl named Natasha. Amanda, the shelter coordinator, had each of moms introduce themselves and their little ones. Natasha, who goes by Tasha, was eighteen and had a little boy named Zach. After the introductions, Amanda turned the tables and had all the prospective mentors introduce themselves to the single moms. Then she invited the group to mingle and get to know one another.

As Joy sat there listening to each teenager, there was something about Tasha's story and how she talked about it that drew Joy to her. She was direct and plainspoken and wasn't really trying to impress anyone. It seemed like she really didn't need a mentor, but she indicated in her introduction that she was willing to have one because the house was encouraging them to be mentored. There was a hard edge to her that Joy found herself attracted to. She didn't know why, but as she met the other girls, it was Tasha who made the biggest impression on her. It wasn't so much that she didn't need anyone, but there was some kind of earnestness about her, a stubbornness to play by the rules, that was remarkably authentic. It was refreshing to Joy.

Once the evening was over, Amanda asked the mentors to email her to let her know which girls they would be interested in mentoring. Joy got home and immediately emailed Amanda indicating that she was drawn to Tasha and wanted the opportunity to walk with her through this time of her life if she was willing.

The following weekend, Joy got an email back from Amanda indicating that Tasha was willing to meet with her, and gave her Tasha's email so they could set up a time to meet.

The day rolled around, and Joy pulled up to the house and walked in to pick up Tasha. She was waiting in the living room of the house and greeted Joy with a warm smile.

"I was hoping that we would be able to do this. Thanks for stepping up, Joy. I really appreciate it." Tasha seemed far more relaxed than the last time Joy talked to her. Little wonder, they had all been on edge, as they were just meeting each other for the first time.

"Absolutely, Tasha. It's my pleasure and honor to do so!" Joy replied. "Anywhere in particular you want to go?"

"It sounds completely crazy, but I would absolutely love a Chick-fil-A milk shake." Tasha smiled as she described it.

"Any particular flavor you are longing for?" Joy asked, chuckling at Tasha's description.

"Cookies and cream is my drop-dead favorite!" Tasha answered Joy almost before the question escaped her mouth.

"Okay! You're on. Let's head out." Joy turned to head for the car, and Tasha followed her.

They chatted about various things about Tasha's life before Zach came along, and they were laughing about the cravings during pregnancy, comparing how weird each woman's cravings can be. Then suddenly Tasha was quiet as they pulled into the parking lot and walked in. They got their orders and walked over to an empty table.

Joy looked at her without touching her milk shake and said, "Tasha, what happened back there? You shut down on me all of a sudden. What's going on?"

"I'm afraid to ask, Miss Joy," Tasha replied, all of a sudden looking like a little girl ready to run out the door.

"Help me out here, Tasha. I would really like to know. It's okay, you won't hurt my feelings or anything. Really, it's okay," Joy said softly.

"Well, it dawned on me, how did you know about pregnancy like that? Did you have a baby too?" She looked down while she talked.

"Well, actually, yes, I did, Tasha. I knew about that because it is all pretty fresh for me still. Now, listen, what I'm about to tell you isn't to make you feel bad at all, you understand?" Joy held her gaze.

Tasha nodded tentatively.

"I had a baby about a year ago, and when I realized that my baby had stopped moving, I went to the doctor. I found out that my little boy had died during that week before I gave birth. So, when he was born, I had to say good-bye in the same day. I'm still trying to recover from it all, but I must say it did me good to laugh about some of the worst days I had being pregnant. So, thanks for that." Joy's face brightened as she looked at Tasha.

"Oh, I am so sorry, Joy. I didn't know. It now makes sense why you would know all that stuff. I had an aunt who lost a baby, and she was really broken up about it for a long time. I can't begin to imagine Zach not being part of my life, no matter how hard it is and how I've been disowned by my family," Tasha replied.

She continued, "Hope House was a real lifesaver for me and Zach. We were out on the street for a couple of months, and it was really bad. I think it's a miracle that we are here. One of the things they do is have someone come in and talk to us girls once a week. One lady talked about how sometimes we have people to make deposits in us just so we can be ready for when there is a withdrawal, like the pain and sorrow of losing people or like what you went through. It isn't the deposit that's the problem, but the withdrawal when we have to take out against what little we might have. It's funny. I didn't plan on getting pregnant, and I thought when I got the news that there was no way I would have enough for a little baby. What I didn't know was that love has a way of compounding as we give it away to people we love." She paused.

"Wow, Tasha, that's really beautiful. I have never heard it said that way. Thanks for sharing that with me. Look at you! You're helping me more than I'm helping you, all for the cost of a milk shake!" Joy laughed.

—⁂—

By the time we enter the fall of our grief, we have been in long seasons of small deposits being made into our lives by key people. That includes wisdom, encouragement, empathy, and companionship. Eventually, there comes a time when we begin to feel that it's time to make some withdrawals from the investments people have made in our lives in order to help others. That is exactly what Joy is doing by stretching herself into another relationship that holds some significant wrinkles in it but that will allow her to see God redeem her pain and sorrow from her loss. It's far from easy to do this, as there is a certain resistance toward taking risks in new relationships where we could lose someone we love again. However, what we don't see is what has been happening to those deposits people have made over the long seasons of winter, spring, and summer. They have not only compounded, but they have increased our courage to risk relationships again.

34

A Matter of Loyalty

*"Loyalty means nothing unless it has at its heart
the absolute principle of self-sacrifice."*
—Woodrow Wilson

As time passed, Joy and Tasha got closer and closer. Joy genuinely looked forward to seeing Tasha each week. But there was one issue that prompted her to tap on the brakes, and he had a name. It was little Zach. When the weather was not too hot, Joy and Tasha went to a city park not far from the house with Zach.

"How's the week been, Tasha?" Joy asked as they sat down on a bench. The moment Tasha put Zach down, he toddled out onto the playground. Tasha answered with a watchful eye on Zach as he played with the wood chips that made up the playground's floor.

"Well, after I got done with school, I picked up Zach from the in-school day care, and I stopped by the coffee shop to see if I could get a job application. I got one and came home. Once Zach went down for his nap, I looked it over, and I don't know. I just feel so unprepared and unskilled to do a job like that," Tasha said, shaking her head.

"I guess that's pretty understandable given how a pregnancy can kind of put us out of commission for a while," Joy replied.

"It is that, but more so. It feels like another reminder that I'm just not ready for any of this . . . being a mom, getting a job, and even trying to live on my own. I feel like such a failure." Tasha looked dejected and discouraged.

"I'm so sorry, Tasha. I certainly can understand that. Trying to raise a baby is a huge responsibility even for people much older than you. I think you're really brave for keeping Zach and now moving back into life. That is far from easy." Joy touched her shoulder to comfort her.

"I don't feel very brave, Joy," Tasha answered. She saw Zach starting to look at the wood chips like they were dinner. She darted toward Zach and caught his hand just before he took a mouthful of the wood chips.

"Yuck, Zach! That's not for eating!" Zach accepted the correction, dropped the handful of chips, and wagged his little head back and forth as if to reprimand himself.

As Joy watched the interaction, she recognized that her heart ached watching it. If only she had had the opportunity to do that with her own son.

Tasha came back to the stroller and fished out some toys for Zach, then sat down near him.

After a while, Tasha looked over at Joy and said, "Joy, I've really got to go to the bathroom. Would you mind watching him until I get back? It'll only take a minute."

Almost before Joy could consider her response, she said, "Sure, I'd be glad to." She went and sat down near Zach and started to engage him with the toy truck he was playing with. It felt like an out-of-body experience where she was watching herself play with little Zach. She felt a huge amount of ambivalence and felt like screaming to her other self, *Don't get too close! You'll lose him too!*

She did keep her emotional distance while making sure he was okay, and before long Tasha came back and took over.

The next morning she took her almost-daily walk with Meg. She spent the first leg of their walk describing what had happened at the playground.

"So, help me understand what the ambivalence was all about, Joy?" Meg was just turning a corner, so her voice trailed off at the end.

"Wait, what did you ask, Meg? I didn't hear it all." Joy quickly caught up and looked over at Meg.

"Oh sorry, I've taken this route so many times alone, I end up talking in front of me instead to whoever's beside me." Meg smiled. She repeated her question.

"I guess I really wanted to bond with Zach just to be a good friend to Tasha, but it felt like I was being disloyal to Aaron. I didn't count on something like that pushing so many buttons. I mean, Zach didn't do anything wrong; it was all me," Joy replied, shaking her head in confusion and frustration.

"You know, Joy, after Frank died, it took me a long time to allow other relationships into my life, particularly men. As much as we hear that we need to reinvest in life, it just feels like we are abandoning the person we love. Almost like I gave the person all the love I had and didn't have any more to give. I felt like it was either Frank had all my love or no one would have it. When he died, he took all my love with him. I had nothing else to give to anyone else." Meg looked back at Joy.

"Yeah, I guess that was it. It was my loyalty to Aaron that held me back from Zach. Does that get any better, Meg?"

"Yes, it does, but at times it feels like quite a hill to climb, and that sense of loyalty is tough to overcome. What you will eventually sort out is that we can be loyal to more than one person. The only difference is that our loyalty to the person we have lost stays static because they never change after the last day we saw them. The loyalty we develop for other people in our lives changes and deepens because we change and those other people change, which impacts the level of loyalty we have toward them."

They finished their walk, and Joy found she had a lot to think about before meeting with Tasha and Zach.

One of the toughest challenges in the fall of our grief is that in spite of the world feeling like it has come alive with new colors of life and vibrancy, with that transition come opportunities to invest in new relationships. As we move into those relationships, we bump into this sense of disloyalty we feel by investing in other relationships. We have to find some way to settle this in our own minds. Sometimes it requires writing another letter like we talked about in earlier chapters, just to explain to the person who is gone the changes we are making. Placing ourselves in suspended animation when it comes to relationships is not a testimony to the depth and richness we may have experienced in the relationship with our lost loved one. Actually, allowing ourselves the freedom to move into new relationships is just as important, and we have to recognize that the influence of the person we have lost is actually responsible for equipping us for the new relationships. Keeping both relationships important in our hearts creates a depth that we would otherwise not have known, and this depth will show up in our future relationships. We can't see it, but people who interact with us will experience our depth, our compassion, our empathy, and our faithfulness because of the influence of those we've lost.

35

BECOMING DEEPER

*"The depth of darkness to which you can descend
and still live is an exact measure of the height to which
you can aspire to reach."*
—Pliny the Elder

Joy was taking her walk on this day alone because Meg was busy with family activities. She grabbed her earbuds and phone and headed out the door. She had no particular direction in mind, but once she found a comfortable stride, she started to think about her relationship with Tasha and Zach and felt puzzled over the fact that she was having feelings at all. She felt as if it was high time for her to move on and get back into life again. Of course, when she made the move to do that, she was hit with conflicting feelings of sorrow, disloyalty, and a sense of abandoning her little boy. Right on the heels of those thoughts, Joy reminded herself that this journey through grief was her own and she didn't need to hold out the "I should be over this by now" poster in her head. She had to keep telling herself that there were going to be regressions during this journey and that some seasons were going to crash into one another. It was never going to be that clean and not messy.

As she walked, suddenly her audiobook app stopped and her phone rang. She looked down at the caller ID and saw that it was Phoebe, with whom she had visited her son's grave only a few months prior.

"Hey, Phoebe! Long time no talk! How's it going and to what do I owe the pleasure of a phone call?" Joy said brightly.

"Hi, Joy! I was just on a break between block classes, and I was thinking about you so I thought I would call you to see how it was going. The last time we spent time together was pretty rough. I only regret I didn't check on you sooner. Sorry!" Phoebe replied.

"Don't sweat it, Phoebe. I understand completely. Actually it has been quite an eventful ten months since we went to the cemetery." Joy was busy concentrating on crossing the street without getting hit while also trying to compose a coherent sentence for her friend. It was a particularly busy street, so it needed her full attention.

"Hang on a sec, Phoebe. I've got to cross Sullivan Road, and it's particularly busy, so I'd better concentrate."

"Take your time, Joy. I'm not going anywhere!"

When Joy finally got across the street safely, she picked up the conversation. "Okay . . . now, where was I? Oh yeah, it's been an eventful ten months or so. Listen, would you be interested in getting coffee again soon so we can catch up?"

"Sure, I'm glad you asked because that was why I was calling—to get together. When and where?" Phoebe responded.

"How about this coming Friday at ten a.m.?" Joy answered.

"You're on. I'll see you then!" Phoebe hung up, and Joy went back to her walk.

When Friday came, Phoebe and Joy met at the same coffee shop they had debriefed after their cemetery visit.

"So, Joy, you said it has been an eventful last few months. What did that mean?" Phoebe smiled thinking how good it was to see her friend again. She noticed that Joy seemed noticeably happier and much more animated than when she had seen her last.

"Yeah, I've been seeing my counselor off and on and hanging out with Meg, a family friend who has also had a significant loss herself. She's been a wonderful voice of wisdom for me," Joy replied.

"That's great, Joy! You seem so different from the last time we met."

"Really, how so?" Joy asked.

"I don't know, you just seem lighter, not so deeply bothered by what was going on in your heart, which makes complete sense given how close you were to losing Aaron. The interesting thing about it, though, is that you seem deeper, like you've gone deep in your relationship with God and with people. You seem less restless than you were even before Aaron came into your life. I would say that you have looked death in the face and grown. It's truly a transformation that I see in your reactions and your thoughtfulness." Phoebe seemed to be struggling to find the words to convey what she had noticed.

It was comforting for Joy to hear Phoebe say these things because from her interactions with Tasha and Zach, Joy had been feeling like she hadn't gotten anywhere.

"You flatter me, Phoebe. I'm thankful for what you said because just lately I've been talking to a young single mom and her little boy, Zach. I've actually been feeling like I haven't gotten anywhere in this journey through my grief," Joy responded.

"Really? What do you mean, Joy?" Phoebe looked over at her with a genuinely quizzical look on her face.

"Oh, I don't know. I had an interaction with Zach the other day while Tasha was gone only briefly, and I really held back from getting attached to him. I was battling fears of losing him, too, if I got too attached. It would have been so simple to pick him up and play with him, but I felt the uncertainty in my heart about it." Joy wondered to herself why she wasn't able to do that.

"Well, first of all, before I talk about that, let me point something out. Remember when I said that you have become deep?" Phoebe looked over at her.

"Yeah . . ." Joy's voice trailed off; she felt like she was in two places at once, remembering that moment with Zach and trying to tune in to Phoebe.

"The fact that you have that level of self-reflection is an indication of how and how much you have grown. To notice the hesitation in your heart like that is nothing short of remarkable. Something has had to happen for you to notice, and then use that as something important to reflect on."

She continued, "Secondly, remember when you said that Meg told you about grief being like seasons?" She waited for Joy's response.

"Yeah . . ." This time Joy was beginning to connect the dots that Phoebe was pointing to.

"It seems to me that this is a pretty good example of that. The thoughts of summer are still present during the fall of your grief. One season overlaps or intrudes on another. Make sense?" She looked expectantly at Joy.

"I guess I forgot that little detail. Go figure, right?" Joy's expression lightened as she felt more encouraged than she had in a few days.

Once we get to fall, it is easy to lapse into the thinking that it's "clear sailing" from here. But seasons continue to overlap and intrude onto one another. All we have to do is look ahead and see what the next season is—winter, right? The encouragement and lightness we feel during the fall collides with the encroaching winter with its anniversaries and other memories that were part of our first winter of grief. But we are different this time. We have grown and deepened, as Phoebe described Joy. That allows us to weather the storms that will no doubt come as we head into the next seasons of our grief journey.

36

THIS IS WHAT HEALING
LOOKS LIKE?

"Healing doesn't mean the damage never existed.
It means the damage no longer controls your life."
—Akshay Dubey

So this is what recovery from the grief of losing Aaron looks like? No one ever told me that there were so many losses even after the most awful one anyone can experience.

Joy was back in her journal once again. She hadn't been there for quite some time, but she thought, given the events of the last month or so, it would be helpful to sort out for herself what had been happening with Zach considering what Phoebe had said to her when they met for coffee.

I guess I thought that healing would be the absence of the feelings I had when Aaron died. Yet it seems that it has been the intensifying of them, in some ways. In other ways, the feelings have gotten reorganized somehow. I guess the accumulation of input from friends like Meg, Phoebe, Lauren, and even the catastrophic interactions with the girls have all helped me to rethink a lot of the thoughts and feelings I had before any of this ever happened. The one thing I have noticed is that the more I move back into life, it feels like I am moving away from my devotion and love for Aaron. It feels like another loss of him. This time it is the loss of the pain I felt in losing him. As if my pain was what connected me to him. Actually, if I were honest, just after Aaron died, since I began this journey (very reluctantly, I might add), it seems like the path has taken me further and further away from him. And with each step, I have found myself fighting it because another step means losing more of him. I realize that that's how it feels to me, but the one thing I have learned is that those feelings are every bit as valid as the thoughts and beliefs I have developed over the last year or so. Not that one is more important than another; they are just different and even in some ways complement each other in terms of my whole experience of Aaron.

I guess the question is, Am I losing Aaron, or am I just taking him with me into the future? At the beginning of my grief, I was clinging on to anything I could because each memory, each feeling, even each role I played were all attached to him, and that was the only way to stay connected to him. What I'm finding out is that my attachment to him is changing. It used to feel like I was forgetting him, but what I'm actually doing is building a space in my heart for him to always reside—because he will.

Now, let me reflect on my relationship with Zach and Tasha. It feels to me that Zach is just like what Aaron would have been. I know that's not true, but it seems that God has placed Zach in my life to show me what hope looks like, and to remind me that hope didn't die when Aaron died. I'm realizing that hope isn't based on a desired outcome but on what happens on the journey to that outcome. Do I wish I could have been at the park with Tasha and Zach with Aaron? Absolutely! But the fact that Aaron is in my heart rather than with me in person doesn't make him any less important. He has given to me, his mom, more than I could have ever given to him in a lifetime. It's strange that in his death, my whole life has been changed. Looking at those words I just wrote, I would have said I was out of my mind, but to me they feel solid and true, and something that creates a well of love and compassion for little kids like Zach whose lives I'm given the opportunity to be a part of. I now see why Jesus took such delight in children. They are God's gift of an embodied redemption from the evil we live with every day. They are innocence, hope, expectation, even life. Even in death, Aaron gave me life and more love than I could have ever imagined.

Joy paused as she thought back over the last year or so.

There is a significance that cannot be overstated in the journal entry above. Look back to the first few installments of Joy's journey, and you will be able to see a remarkable transformation has taken place. The thing to keep in mind is that this journey of Joy's has been far from an easy stroll to her recovery from her grief. Actually, that is exactly the nature of scars that we all have on our bodies. Scars usually tell stories of pain, disappointment, heartache, and eventual healing. If you ask anyone about a particular scar on their body, you will usually hear how they got the scar. Sometimes what happened was pretty dramatic, but looking at them in the moment, you would have never known. That is very much what grief is like. There is a dramatic wound that has occurred, the loss of someone we love, and then we embark on the journey into healing, but there are always twists and turns, and regressions, and remarkable progress made during that journey. We don't count on bumps in the road and can often get discouraged by them, even making the mistake of believing that the bumps in the road, rather than the progress we have made, define our journey through grief.

The fall of our grief, much like the fall season in nature, marks a significant transition in our world. The burst of colors is a signal that the colors will fade into winter again. Our temptation is to define the whole year by the loss of color to winter instead of looking back on the journey and seeing just how far we have come—and celebrating! The key to remember about any of the seasons of grief we pass through is that there will be intrusions and interruptions that are completely normal for the journey. And just remember, those interruptions do not define the entire journey; in fact, they might actually be opportunities to reflect and consider not only where we have been but also the journey ahead. Be patient with yourself. Be gentle with yourself, and allow yourself the grace to grow through some of the toughest parts of being human and loving deeply.

37

LOSING THE SHADOW

"The reality is that you will grieve forever. You will not 'get over' the loss of a loved one; you will learn to live with it. You will heal and you will rebuild yourself around the loss you have suffered. You will be whole again but you will never be the same. Nor should you be the same nor would you want to."
—Elizabeth Kubler-Ross and David Kessler

After Aaron died and Joy held him her arms in the hospital, she said good-bye for the last time. It seemed that a shadow had moved into her life as well. As time passed, it seemed to lurk on the edge of Joy's journey through grief as a companion that she simply couldn't shake. At times, when she was missing Aaron the most and mourning the things she wished he could've experienced, the shadow grew more intense and near. She realized over her journey that the more she looked to the future, the less intrusive the shadow seemed to become, but there was something about it that was a comforting presence after Aaron died. She realized that would sound strange to anyone else, but it seemed that the shadow was a reminder that something really awful had happened, and allowing the shadow in her life was one way to recognize it.

As she was investing more and more into her relationship with Tasha and Zach, something surprising happened. She began to realize that she really didn't need the shadow anymore to validate the importance of the loss of Aaron in her life. It was her investment in her life that actually accomplished that.

She didn't really know what to do with the shadow or how to make it go away once and for all. She decided to visit her counselor again to have a needed check-up.

She was able to get an appointment with Tricia fairly quickly.

Joy entered Tricia's office and immediately felt that sense of peace and tranquility that it had offered her when she was in the throes of her grief. Tricia gave her a hug in greeting.

"It is so good to see you, Joy. So, catch me up. How's it going, and what brings you in today?" Tricia said as she settled into her chair.

"Well, I must say it has been a full and eventful six months since I saw you last, Tricia. You'll be glad to hear that I have begun to invest in life again and have made some pretty big adjustments to living life. For example, I was compelled to start helping at a home for single moms, and I'm mentoring a young mom named Tasha and her little boy named Zach. It's been stretching to say the least." Joy paused because she could tell that Tricia was about to burst.

"Oh my gosh, Joy! I'm so proud of you. You're making quite the strides in traversing the seasons of your grief. Well done!" Tricia was grinning from ear to ear.

"Yeah, thanks. I do appreciate it. I thought I would take your reminders at the end of many of our sessions just to get a checkup on how I'm doing. I do have a specific question that I wanted to run by you too."

"Okay, shoot," Tricia replied.

"I don't know how much I talked about it with you, but after Aaron died, I felt like there was a shadow that was always with me. It would just be cast over pretty much anything that I was doing, and at times I actually got pretty comfortable with it because it felt like it was the last remnant I had of

Aaron, and if I lost that, I would lose a little bit more of him." Joy paused to let Tricia absorb what she was saying.

"Well, over the last month or so, and particularly since I started mentoring Tasha, it seems like the shadow is reducing, but I still feel a certain hesitation because I've gotten so comfortable with the shadow. Any thoughts?" Joy looked expectantly at Tricia.

"Ah, you know me, Joy, I always have some thoughts about stuff, right?" Tricia winked at her.

"Yeah, I know, I shouldn't have bothered to ask, but what do you think?" Joy shot back sarcastically.

"The funny thing . . . okay it's not really funny. Irritating, frustrating, and aggravating might be better words to describe it, but in the grief journey there are often echoes of the past that seem to linger for so long. That sounds a little like the shadow you keep referring to. I have heard others say that before, how comforting it is in spite of the fact that it is a constant reminder of who has been lost. In some ways, it is the last vestige of the shadow of grief that we have had with us over the course of our recovery. What I have found is that there comes a moment when someone has to say good-bye to the shadow and actually embrace the memories that are left behind of the person we have lost. The irony that we find out is that the tighter we hold on to the shadow, the more it consumes the very memories we are fighting to keep. The moment we let it go, it seems that we are finally free to embrace those memories, allow them to change and deepen us for future relationships and to give us the courage to try again." Tricia paused to give Joy a chance to digest what she had said. "Okay, it's my turn. What do think or feel about what I said?"

Joy took a deep breath and said, "I suppose a lot of that is a relief to hear. That I'm not going crazy or been doing this grief journey thing wrong this whole time."

Tricia was shaking her head, indicating that wasn't her point at all.

Joy continued, "It just feels like it is time to look to the future, but I don't feel like I am abandoning Aaron by doing so. All this time, it's felt like he has been woven into who I am and how I see myself and my relationship with others. So now, as I move into the future, I'm taking him with me and also giving away to someone like Zach a little deposit of what Aaron gave me."

"That's truly beautifully said, Joy. I couldn't have said it any better!" Tricia was smiling.

When the appointment was over, Joy was rolling over in her mind what she was going to do. She got home, grabbed her journal, and headed for the back deck.

My dear little boy,

Oh, how I miss you. I met a little boy who is older than you would've been, but I'm sure you would have loved playing with him. This past year has been the hardest I have ever faced in my life. And you have gotten me through it. I don't think I can ever love anyone as much as I have loved you, but I'm willing to find out. You have been woven into my very soul, and you are even now giving me the courage to go into the future without you and even to risk loving someone else again.

Good-bye little one. You will always be with me, and I can't wait to see you again, but it's time for me to move into the future with all that you have given me. I love you and always will. Until we meet again.

—Your mom

CONCLUSION

"Grief is like a long valley, a winding valley where any bend may reveal a totally new landscape."

—C.S. Lewis

Stories often mark a beginning and an end. While Ben's and Joy's stories come to an end in this book, there is another beginning waiting not only for them (in spite of the fact that they are fictional) but for us as well. Their stories have described a path of grief, loss, discouragement, despair, and unexpected joys. Their journeys give you a rare look into the "nuts and bolts" of the grief process.

I would encourage you to use their stories to underscore the importance of grieving in your life. Not only is it our reaction to the loss we have experienced, but it is also our way to honor the importance of the people in our lives. Sadly, we have lost the value of lament in our lives. It is almost as if we want our lives only to be mountaintops and rainbows. While we know that is not realistic, we impose such a perspective on our expectations of how life is supposed to be rather than learning how to live the life we have. What many fail to discover is that all of life is the acceptance of the reality we are in, not the illusion that we hope it to be. Our acceptance of it is not our approval of the bad things that we experience; it is a willingness to adapt to that which is hard, heart-wrenching, and thoroughly human. In so doing, we become the "deep" people that this world so profoundly needs.

My hope in writing a book like this is that rather than being taught something about grief and its seasons, you will have a better idea, by watching the stories of others, of how the process of grieving goes. The grieving process is far from bloodless, as often books on grieving unintentionally make it sound. It is messy, frustrating, confusing, and even fulfilling. There are critical characteristics to the seasons we walk through that I have given you a brief glimpse of. There is no formula to follow. The grieving process invites us to trust the One who has created us for connection, and when that connection is broken, we very naturally rebel. We *should* rebel. Unfortunately, we will despise the impulse for connection rather than rebel against the stain that loss brings into our lives unbidden and uninvited. It is not our ache and hunger for connection that is the problem; it is our losses that are a difficult and cruel reminder of the broken world in which we live.

As you look ahead at your journey through the seasons of your grief, I would encourage you to give yourself permission to experience your grief fully because it is a memorial to the love you have for the person you have lost. Don't apologize for your tears or your pain. Allow your pain to breathe, don't condemn it, and in time when the fall of your grief appears, you might be surprised that the hated companion of grief has faded from view. At this point, you will have walked the difficult road of being human and experiencing loss. You will have continued the journey, and while grief will no longer be with you at this point of your journey, it will come to visit you through the years to come. This time, though, it will be a visit from an "old" companion who is not dreaded but accepted. With that acceptance, you will begin to find that his visits become shorter and shorter—not unexpected but recognized for the role he (grief) has played in your life. As old friends always do, he leaves again and your life goes on.

About the Author

In 2005, after experiencing a devastating accident that left him in perpetual pain, Dr. Mitsch embarked on a journey into the heart of God realizing that God didn't need him to accomplish ministry for Him. Dr. Mitsch was hijacked by the tender, relentless grace of Jesus that cemented his conviction that God wanted a brutally honest, authentic relationship with him. This led him into a long desert experience with God that has refined and transformed his relationships and his relationship with his Abba.

Dr. Mitsch has been in the counseling profession since 1980. In 1993 he started his own counseling practice called Cornerstone Counseling Center and has been in private practice since that time. He has had extensive experience in men's ministry and caring ministries within the local church.

Dr. Mitsch has used his forty years of experience in working with missionaries from around the world. As a result, he has had the opportunity to work with over a thousand missionary families both on the field as well as on home assignment. He has been actively involved in field-based crisis intervention, candidate assessment, and post-field debriefing as well as trauma debriefing.

He founded a tax-exempt nonprofit organization called Stained Glass International (sgi-net.org) devoted to reaching out to Generation Z, who are fleeing away from the church at an alarming rate. This organization, which includes *The Outpost Podcast*, is committed to equipping, empowering, and encouraging the next generation of young people in their relationship with Jesus and each other.

He has authored five books, including his best-selling book *Grieving the Loss of Someone You Love*, selling over four hundred thousand copies worldwide. He was a charter member of the American Association of Christian Counseling and is a licensed psychologist in Colorado. Ray has been married to Linda for forty-four years and blessed to have four daughters—Corrie, Anne, Abigail, and Elizabeth—and three grandsons—Greyson, Desmond, and Henry. The Mitsches live in the Denver area.

NOTES

1. William Nicholson, *Shadowlands*, directed by Richard Attenborough (Price Entertainment, 1993), 01:46:50.
2. Shakespeare, William, *Macbeth: In Plain and Simple English (A Modern Translation and the Original Version) (Classics Retold: 4)* (Anaheim, CA: Golgotha Press, 2013), loc. 2968 of 3680, Kindle.